RESTRUCTURING AS A PATHWAY TO UNITY AND DEVELOPMENT

The Atiku Abubakar Files

RESTRUCTURING AS A PATHWAY TO UNITY AND DEVELOPMENT

The Atiku Abubakar Files

POLAF
POLITICAL AFRICA INITIATIVE

ISBN: 978-978-55255-3-3

Published in Nigeria in 2017 by Narrative Landscape Press for Political Africa Initiative (POLAF)
info@polaf.org
www.polaf.org

Cover Design by Black and Lee Creative Hub
Text Layout by Shobola Ibukun
Photo Credits: Google Images

TABLE OF CONTENTS

"Although our interests as citizens vary, each one is an artery to the heart that pumps life through the body politic, and each is important to the health of democracy."

Bill Moyers

INTRODUCTION

Healthy democracies can only thrive in the presence of incessant and keen debates. More importantly, they are sustained when all players - from diverse backgrounds, religions, culture and ethnicity cast off their dichotomies, in united pursuit of an overarching purpose. Concerning democracy, American statesman and 32nd president, Franklin Roosevelt, notes:

"Democracy, of all forms of government, enlists the full force of men's enlightened will."

The force of enlightened will is what lends credence to unrestricted exhibition of freedoms. In Nigeria, this reality stares both leaders and citizens in the face. The clamoring from different quarters testifies to this. The disenfranchisement of various sections of the Nigerian nation has continued to intensify since the departure from military rule to democracy. This is not to say that democracy is the cause of the clamoring; it is to note however, that democracy has served as a megaphone for the often ignored dissenting voices whispering underneath for years, burdened by military rule. Democracy indeed has given voice to the voiceless.

One thing synonymous with advanced nations is the existence of political and economic structures which provide enabling environment for growth, development and welfare of the citizenry. In Nigeria, much is left to be desired with respect to these, and has led to the pronounced bedlam and upheavals. Undoubtedly, Nigeria's democracy still qualifies as fledgling hence much room exists for improvement. Indisputably, every living thing panders to change, for improvement. Grow or blow. Expand or extinct. Nothing living stagnates. At the state of prolonged stagnation, restlessness sets in. This also explains the state of chaos in the nation.

The issues of prevalent poverty, dearth of infrastructure, marginalization and many others, need to be urgently addressed. Nigeria cannot afford apathy and indifference; being proactive is essential to keeping sanity as a nation. Truly, Nigeria in no way lacks the means or capacity to address these issues. The wherewithal is available. Unfortunately, the country's gross domestic income, which has been majorly from oil and gas, has suffered setbacks in recent times, due to fall in oil prices globally. The oil boom largesse that made us neglect agriculture is almost leaving us stranded. In the face of present economic downturn, we have been forced to diversify the economy via agriculture, solid mineral exports, small and medium scale enterprises, and so on. Yet this is not enough.

It appears like the fundamental framework and platform on which the very existence and workings of national governance rest need to be revisited. The present lopsided federal structure of Nigeria is arguably the harbinger of underdevelopment and a major contributory factor to the political conflicts that assail the country. The cries of marginalization, as well as the undeniable stagnation in national progress and development, implore Nigerians to lend a listening ear to the proposition of restructuring the existing federal structure. When a system is not delivering expected results and outcomes, the logic is to either change it entirely or innovate. Nigeria desperately needs a new structure that fosters freedoms and government accountability, restructures electoral laws, and decentralizes powers to states and local governments, as is consistent with genuine federal systems. But the long road to restructuring might not be an easy one to tread.

This book, Restructuring as a Pathway to Unity and Development which is a compilation of speeches delivered by former Nigerian vice president, Atiku Abubakar as well as his contributory pieces published in some Nigerian Newspapers, highlights and addresses the persistent and recurring challenges experienced in key sectors of the nation. Touching on virtually all segments of national life, at different fora, sundry audiences and in diverse locations nationwide – North, East, West and South, Atiku Abubakar's ideas, as clearly expressed in this collection, attempt to entrench fiscal federalism and local control of resources (with federal taxing powers). Atiku's plea for the restructuring of Nigeria's federal system is in tandem with his political and economic ideologies.

Restructuring as a Pathway to Unity and Development does not attempt to paint restructuring of the federal structure as being able to help us entirely surmount all obstacles confronting Nigeria's democratic progression but persuades that it can serve as a durable framework from which a fresh trajectory can ensue for all sectors of national life and at the same time further establish Nigeria's democracy.

Central Mosque

"None of us is as Great As All of Us"

Atiku Abubakar

PREFACE

The number one problem plaguing Nigeria is not corruption or even the absence of regular power. The number one problem militating against the progress of Nigeria is her lack of unity. If we can fix this problem, Nigeria will herself be fixed.

In the Bible, God spoke about mankind in Genesis 11:6 thus, "If as one people speaking the same language they have begun to do this, then nothing they plan to do will be impossible for them." Similarly, the Holy Quran, also states, "Do not quarrel among yourselves lest you lose heart and your momentum disappear." Quran 8:46

From the above, it is clear that we can never have a Nigeria that fulfils her full potential when we have a divided Nigeria. Not only will we lose momentum as the Quran shows us, we will also lose our possibilities as the Bible teaches us.

An objective look at history will show that without exception, all nations or regions that have expelled people from their landmass on the basis of race, religion or political affiliation have been the poorer for it, whether you are talking of the Alhambra Decree which purged Jews from Spain in 1492, or of more recent events like the purge of Asians from Uganda in 1972.
Nigerians may recall the 'Ghana Must Go' purge of 1983, which led to the forced departure of over a million Ghanaians from Nigeria. Nigeria lost many skilled workers and small businesses when the Ghanaians left. But they went home and developed their country and today, Ghana is the top destination for Nigerians wishing to study abroad.

Because of how these immigrants helped develop and organise their country, there are today over a quarter of a million Nigerians in Ghana and the Ghanaians have now coined the phrase 'Nigerians are Coming' to identify this phenomenon. We must learn from history. We do not have to repeat history. We must learn from the mistakes of other people. As Albert Einstein famously said, "The definition of insanity is doing the same thing over and over again and expecting different results."

It would be insane if a nation that once sang the song of 'Go on With One Nigeria,' should be seen to be singing a new and absurd song of 'Go on Without Some Nigerians'. What that would mean is that the sacrifices of the millions of men, women and children who died in the process of keeping Nigeria one would have been a sacrifice made in vain. This would negate the line in our National Anthem which reads, "The labour of our heroes past shall never be in vain."

It will be an even greater shame that if after we all were united to condemn the xenophobic attacks in South Africa, now hypocritically turn around and treat our own kith and kin even worse. We have six geopolitical zones in Nigeria and I was one of those, who participated in bringing this about at the 1995 Constitutional Conference. The reasoning behind this is the awareness that none of us is as great as all of us.

Our six zones each have six strengths, but our one Nigeria together has six hundred strengths. You do not believe me? Look at the different Nigerian football teams that won the Olympic gold medal, the Africa Cup of Nations, the maiden edition of FIFA U-17 World Cup in 1985, and the team that qualified for our very first FIFA World Cup in 1994. It took a combination of Nigerians from all zones to pull these feats. The struggle of Nigeria in 2017 is not a struggle between North and South; rather, it is a struggle between good and evil.

It would not be possible for Nigeria to exist as one corporate entity, comprising the six geopolitical zones, if this were not the plan of God. If this is the plan of the Almighty, and it evidently is, then whose plan would it be to cause division in what God has united?

"What therefore God has joined together, let not man put asunder." Matthew 19:6

Let us think long and deep on this.

A while ago, Emanuel Cleaver said there is more power in unity than in division. Some very clever people may have discovered ways in which they can divide Nigeria, but I am convinced that there are intelligent geniuses and patriots amongst our people, who can discover ways to unite Nigeria and defeat their evil plans.

One of such people is Immaculata Onuigbo, a young Nigerian from Enugu, who was recruited by the Shehu Musa Yar'Adua Foundation, at the very young age 10 and given a scholarship which eventually saw her emerge as the best graduating student of the American University of Nigeria, Yola, with the highest cumulative grade point average score in the school's history. People like Miss Onuigbo are the future of Nigeria and the world, a product of pan-Nigerian collaboration.

Incidentally, she was discovered in Enugu, that great metropolis that in 1956 elected a Northerner, Umaru Altine, as its first elected mayor. It is our history, encapsulated in Umaru Altine and our future in Immaculata Onuigbo that Nigeria needs.

Kano Durbar

"The ballot is stronger than the bullet."

Abraham Lincoln

1 CONSENSUS BUILDING FOR ELECTORAL REFORM

At the National Conference on Consensus Building for Electoral Reform Abuja, 16 July, 2009

I feel honoured to have been asked to contribute to these discussions towards building a national consensus for the reform of our electoral system. I thank the organizers, Centre for Democracy and Development (CDD), the International Republican Institute (IRI) and the National Democratic Institute (NDI), who have helped to sponsor it.

This is one of those gatherings that you wished you did not have to attend because the events and developments that brought our country to the current sorry situation, which necessitated the organizing of this event, were clearly avoidable. But, be that as it may, it is the responsibility of all Nigerians, especially the political leaders, to work hard at ensuring that we take advantage of the small window of opportunity that we must put our electoral system in acceptable order. And we certainly need the assistance of our international friends such as the International Republican Institute, The National Democratic Institute and all the world's mature democracies, as we struggle for electoral democracy in this country.

There are negative and positive incentives for us to work for electoral reforms now. On the negative side is the electoral fraud that we witnessed in the past, and especially in 2007 and continuing through the various re-runs/by-elections. On the positive side are the improvements that electoral reforms would make to our democracy. Consensus building is critical at this historic moment, for the drive for electoral reform to gain momentum. What are the possible terms of that consensus; what should the consensus be based on?

a. I suggest that we can build consensus on the irreducible minimum changes that would ensure genuine electoral reform. Consensus on anything less than genuine electoral reform would not be helpful. It should not be about perfecting Nigeria's electoral system today. If we can secure meaningful electoral reform, one which allows the freely cast votes of Nigerians to count, then we would have embarked on the road to democratic perfection; we would have something to build on.

b. The other critical element is timing. Given our recent horrifying experiences, we must put these reforms in place for the next general elections in 2011. The reforms cannot be put off for a future date. They are needed now.

In broad terms, genuine electoral reforms for this country will be in line with the recommendations of the Electoral Reform Committee (ERC) headed by Honourable Justice Mohammed Uwais. That committee consulted widely across the length and breadth of this country and gathered opinions from Nigerians across the political spectrum. It is our responsibility as Nigerians to resist any attempt to manipulate, dilute or postpone the reforms in ways that render them ineffective. We must have a genuine reform of the electoral system to enable us to freely choose those who will govern us. Without that freedom to choose our leaders, we shall continue to lag dangerously behind as a people. Only genuine reform will be the incentive for political parties, especially the strong ones, to allow internal party democracy. Without it, political godfathers will continue to impose candidates since the votes of the people will not be allowed to count and such leaders would not be accountable to the people.

Genuine electoral reforms must include the following, among other important elements:

1. It must ensure the genuine independence and impartiality of the electoral umpire, the INEC. Thus:

    a. The selection of the Chairman and Board of INEC must be insulated from the government of the day;

    b. Funding for INEC must be a first line charge on the Consolidated Revenue Fund. An electoral umpire that waits for a president to "release" money for its activities or to direct the security agencies to assist it in protecting voters and the ballot is not truly independent. An independent electoral umpire should be able to directly seek the assistance of security agencies, the same way that citizens in a democratic order can seek the lawful assistance and protection of security agencies.

2. While the unbundling of INEC into three separate entities is welcome, the appointment of the heads of those three agencies should be in line with the recommendations of the ERC report regarding the appointment of the Chairman of the INEC. In the future, we should further improve our electoral system, including scrapping the federal electoral umpire all together, so that improved State Independent Electoral Commissions and their equivalents at the local government level should handle all elections. I believe that efforts at making the INEC independent should be extended to the State Independent Electoral Commissions (SIECs) to improve their performance. Scrapping the State Independent Electoral Commissions and centralizing the electoral umpire, as the ERC Report and government white paper recommend, not only erodes our principle of federalism but would make it easier for a ruling party to coordinate rigging across the country.

3. The reform must ensure that votes are counted and the tallies announced at the polling stations and certified copies of the results given to party and security agents. Without a doubt, it would be more difficult to write false results and engage in fraudulent collation if all participating political parties/candidates and security agents have the results from each polling station.

4. Genuine electoral reform must ensure that disputes arising from the elections are resolved before the eventual winner takes office. This will help to end impunity. It is unconscionable that individuals whose elections are being contested at the tribunals and courts would assume office and use public resources to fight off the challenges, for nearly as long as they want.

This makes a mockery of democracy and it must stop. A disputed election to a US Senate seat was only resolved recently, eight months after the election took place. Only then was Al Franken, the eventual winner, allowed to seat in the US Senate beside his Democratic Party colleagues. The electoral dispute between Mr. George W. Bush and Mr. Al Gore was resolved before George Bush assumed office as the president. Here at home, the electoral dispute between Alhaji Shehu Shagari and Chief Obafemi Awolowo was resolved by the courts before Shagari was sworn in as president. That was the requirement of the law in the Second Republic. We must bring it back.

5. Genuine electoral reform must ensure the independence of the security forces, such as the police, in election matters. This requires changes in the manner of the appointment of the Inspector-General of the Police and the issuance of directives to the police and other security forces on election matters. And, as I already pointed out, the electoral umpire should be able to seek the assistance of security agencies without recourse to the president.

6. Let me emphasize that these retorms must be implemented before the 2011 elections. They cannot be put off for a future date; they are needed now. The ERC recommended that elections take place at least six months prior to the swearing in of the eventual winners. This is to enable the tribunals and courts to dispense with cases involving electoral disputes. This means that the next elections should take place latest by November 2010. Again, it means that the reforms must take place now. In addition, we must have a very clear time-table to ensure that what needs to be done is done so that the next elections can take place by November 2010. As a people, we cannot suspend good in order to live with evil for a little while longer. That would be the road to perdition rather than renewal and redemption.

Let us be clear that struggling for these reforms is not about any one individual or group whether or not they have aspired to or are aspiring for elective office. We must look beyond our individual ambitions and interests. It is about our country and its current and future citizens. The durable institutions and processes that we put in place as a result of these reforms will outlive all of us whatever our political affiliations and aspirations. They will enable us and future generations to freely choose those who would govern us and, therefore, make those leaders accountable to the people. Such reforms will help to make our elections meet regional and international standards, gain us international respect and enable us to take our rightful place in the comity of civilized nations.

Distinguished friends, as I wind up, I must stress that the decision of government to reject the recommendation of the Justice Uwais Committee that the National Judicial Council be given the key role of appointing the Chairman of INEC, is self-serving. In the past, the Executive had used arm-twisting tactics to subtly bend the judiciary to submit to its will. It took a protracted struggle to grant the judiciary self-accounting status, that is, financial independence. I recall that at one time, Justice Uwais recommended that an erring judge be dismissed. This was not done for some months until he cried out to the press, which launched a blistering crusade, before the president approved that the erring judge be kicked out.

The bogey of flawed elections has lived with us for a long time and INEC under the Presidency has not been able to rescue the nation from its perpetual bad habit of staging polls which have no integrity. The president has seen the electoral riots in Adamawa, Edo, Ondo and Ekiti, all under his watch. He does not need to continue to concentrate more powers under his canopy, on what I see as purely a technical ground.

Finally, I can say it loud and clear that carpet-crossing has crept back to us through the back door. Governors and legislators have brazenly swapped parties using a loophole in the law, which provides for a quarrel before a legislator can abandon his or her camp for another. This is weak and cries out for amendment. My position is that any politician in office who abandons the platform, on which he or she climbed to office, must go back to the people if he or she changes camp on flimsy grounds. Those who betray the electorate must not profit from their treachery. It has become common for politicians these days to scream on top of their voices that there is no morality in politics or better still, 'Victory first, morality later.' Absolute balderdash! Politics without morality is in fact an absurdity of contradictions, and can only lead to political rascality, and shameless and open abuse of office.

Let me conclude by pleading with President Umaru Yar'Adua to desist from encouraging and receiving carpet-crossers in whatever form or manner they may appear in his party, the PDP. This is especially so since part of his own electoral reform bills sent to the National Assembly include provisions treating such political prostitution or carpet-crossing, after elections, as illegal. The president should be the one leading the crusade of morality in politics, since he is expected to be the moral conscience of the nation.

This is my submission before you, my friends. Thank you for your kind attention, and may God bless the Federal Republic of Nigeria.

National Theatre, Lagos State

"One of the consequences of excessive centralization and the military rule that facilitated it is that the Nigerian President is the most powerful president in the world."

Atiku Abubakar

2 THE URGENT NEED FOR ELECTORAL REFORMS

At the Public Hearings on Electoral Reform by the House of Representatives Committee on Electoral Reforms, Abuja, 11-12 August, 2009

I am very pleased that this honourable committee of the House of Representatives is holding these public hearings on electoral reform, although one would have hoped that the process of reforming our electoral system was being concluded by now, given that time is of the essence.

Nevertheless, it is important that you are holding these hearings on this very important matter. After all is said and done it is your responsibility, Honourable Members, to reform the electoral process through the necessary legislative changes. While some reforms of the electoral process do not require changes to our laws, the most critical ones do and you must act urgently on them now. There is little time to waste; we are almost running behind schedule. As you know, your work is only part of the process. The proposed legislative changes that border on constitutional amendment will have to pass enough State Houses of Assembly to have the force of law, again that will take time. SO, YOU MUST ACT NOW.

We all know what will hasten this process: the government and the ruling party. If the government and the ruling PDP are committed to well-known. I am going to lay them out for this honourable committee to assist you in this important historic work.

Mr. Chairman, Honourable Members, unless we are embarked on another process of deceiving ourselves and our friends, the reform of Nigeria's electoral process must, in broad terms, be in line with the recommendations of the Electoral Reform Committee headed by Honourable Justice Mohammed Lawal Uwais. That committee took great pains to gather the opinions of Nigerians from across this country, from all works of life, and from across the political spectrum. So far, the government has shown little enthusiasm towards implementing the recommendations of that committee. This is certainly not what Nigerians were promised at the inauguration of this administration. And it is not what we were promised at the inauguration of the Electoral Reform Committee. That ERC report must be implemented, if we are to have genuine elections, where the votes of people actually count.

Meaningful electoral reform for this country must contain the following among other important elements:

1. It must guarantee the independence and impartiality of the electoral umpire, the INEC. Therefore:

   a. The appointment of the Chairman and Board of INEC must be insulated from the government of the day;
   a. Funding for the INEC must be a first line charge on the Consolidated Revenue Fund.

   The practice of INEC waiting for a president to "release"

money for its activities or to direct the security agencies to assist it in protecting voters and the ballot is not the mark of an independent agency, A truly independent INEC should be able to directly seek the assistance of security agencies on election matters, the same way that citizens in genuine democracy can seek the lawful assistance and protection of security agencies.

2. I welcome the ERC's recommendation that the INEC be unbundled into three separate entities. However, the appointment of the heads of those three agencies should be in line with the recommendations of the ERC report regarding the appointment of the Chairman of the INEC. In the future, we should explore further improvements of our electoral system, including scrapping the federal electoral umpire all together so that improved State Independent Electoral Commissions and their equivalents at the local level should handle all government elections.

   I believe that efforts at making the INEC independent should be extended to the State Independent Electoral Commissions (SIECs), to improve their performance. To abolish the State Independent Electoral Commissions and centralizing the electoral umpire, as the ERC Report and government white paper recommend, would not only amount to an erosion of our federal structure but would also make it easier for a ruling party to coordinate rigging across the country.

3. Genuine electoral reform for our country must ensure that votes are counted, the tallies announced at the polling stations, and certified copies of the results given to party and security agents. Certainly, it would be more difficult to write false results and engage in fraudulent collation if all participating political parties/candidates and security agents have the results from each polling station.

4. We must stop making a mockery of elections by ensuring that disputes arising from the elections are resolved before the eventual winner takes office. This will help to end impunity. How can we continue to allow individuals whose elections are being contested at the tribunals and courts to assume office and use public resources to fight off the challenges for nearly as long as they want? This must stop.

   Recently, a disputed election to a US Senate seat was finally resolved eight months after the election took place. Only then was Al Franken, the eventual winner, allowed to sit in the US Senate, beside his Democratic Party colleagues. You may recall that the electoral dispute between Mr. George W. Bush and Mr. Al Gore was resolved before George Bush assumed office as the president. You may recall also that the electoral dispute between Alhaji Shehu Shagari and Chief Obafemi Awolowo was resolved by the courts before Shagari was sworn in as President. That was the requirement of the law in the Second Republic. If we are honest and serious, we must bring it back.

5. Genuine electoral reform must ensure the independence of the security forces, such as the police, in election matters. Thus, we must change the manner of the appointment of the Inspector-General of

the Police and the issuance of directives to the police and other security forces on election matters. And, as I already indicated, the INEC should be able to seek the assistance of security agencies without recourse to the President.

6. My Chairman, Honourable Members, it must be stressed that these reforms must be implemented before the 2011 elections. They cannot be put off for a future date; they are needed now. The ERC recommended that the presidential and governorship elections take place at least six months prior to the assumption of office of the eventual winners. This is to enable the tribunals and courts to dispense with cases involving electoral disputes. The implication is that the next governorship and presidential elections should take place latest by November, 2010. Ladies and gentlemen, it means that the reforms must take place now. We must also have a very clear time-table to ensure that the steps that need to be taken are taken so that the next elections can take place by November, 2010. As a people, we must seek renewal and redemption by doing the right things now rather than suspending good in order to live with evil for a little while longer.

7. My dear friends, let me also say, as I conclude, that carpet-crossing has crept back into our political system through the back door. Governors and legislators have brazenly changed parties using a loophole in the law, which provides for a quarrel before a legislator can abandon his or her party for another. This is weak and must be amended. Any politician in office, who abandons the platform on which he or she assumed to office, must go back to the people if he or she changes party on flimsy grounds. Our political system must not reward those who betray the electorate. It has become common for politicians these days to shamelessly say that there is no morality in politics or better still "Victory first, morality later." But politics without morality is in fact an absurdity of contradictions. It can only lead to political rascality, and shameless and brazen abuse of office.

Mr. Chairman, Honourable Members, part of the electoral reform bills sent to the National Assembly by President Umaru Yar'Adua includes provisions that outlaw such post-election political prostitution or carpet-crossing. Is it not proper then to ask the president to desist from encouraging and receiving carpet crossers in whatever form or manner they may appear in his party, the PDP? The president should be the one spearheading the effort to restore morality in politics, since he is supposed to be the moral conscience of the nation.

My dear friends, the struggle for these electoral reforms is not about any one individual or group, whether or not they have aspired to or are aspiring for elective office. It transcends our individual ambitions and interests. It is about our country and its current and future citizens, and it is about how we are viewed by the rest of the world. If we do the right things now, the durable institutions and processes that would result from these reforms will outlive all of us, whatever our political leanings and interests are. Putting in place genuine electoral reforms will enable us and future generations to freely choose those who would govern us and, therefore, make those leaders accountable to the people. Such reforms will help to make our elections meet regional and international standards, earn us international respect and enable us to take our rightful place among civilized nations.

It is in this light that I see the government's rejection of the recommendations of the Justice Uwais Committee that the National Judicial Council be given the key role of appointing the Chairman of INEC, as self-serving and unfortunate indeed. We all know that in the past, the Executive had used arm-twisting tactics to subtly bend the judiciary to submit to its will. It took a sustained struggle to grant the judiciary self-accounting status, that is, financial independence. Today, this country is the better for it.

We have tolerated flawed elections for too long and the INEC under the Presidency has not been able to rescue the nation from its perpetual bad habit of organizing elections which have no integrity whatsoever. We have all witnessed the electoral brigandage in Adamawa, Edo, Ondo and Ekiti, all under watch of the current government. The president does not need to concentrate even more powers in his office on what seems to be purely a technical ground. He must act as a statesman so that this country can realize its full potentials.

Mr Chairman, Honourable Members, this is my submission before you.

Thank you for your kind attention.

May God give you the courage to do the right thing for this country and may God bless the Federal Republic of Nigeria.

Argungu Annual Fishing Festival

"When a nation goes down, or a society perishes, One condition may always be found They forgot where they came from. They lost sight of what had brought them along."

Carl Sandburg

3 THOUGHTS ON THE STRUCTURE OF NIGERIA'S FEDERATION

At the 2012 Leadership Conference & Awards Ceremony Abuja, 18 September, 2012

We have a keynote speaker, so I will take liberties as the chairman, to only make a few remarks on a key issue that has been on the minds of many Nigerians lately, namely the structure of our federation. I believe that it has a bearing on the theme of this important conference. Politics, including opposition politics, is played within the context of the structure of the polity.

I am a product of regional parliamentary democracy. I received free qualitative education from the primary to the secondary and university levels. I was even paid to attend school. The money, which the government of the day, my local authority, used to pay for my education and those of my contemporaries, was not derived from oil revenues. So, I am not a product of the oil boom Nigeria.

I followed a recent debate on the Internet between some American professors and some intellectuals from the Niger Delta and a Northerner. They were trying to answer the question of whether Nigeria or indeed the Niger Delta can be like Singapore. They all agreed that no nation in the world has developed without a combination of its natural resources and human capital. We have natural resources, but without human capital, neither Nigeria nor the Niger Delta can be like Singapore, which did not have significant natural resources to start with. But a nation without natural resources can be like Singapore if it develops its human capital, as Japan did before Singapore.

This is an important lesson for all of us. We must, therefore, demand good governance at all levels of our government. The immense developmental strides achieved by our First Republic leaders were achieved without oil revenues, yet we have for over forty years now been behaving as though nothing can be achieved without oil revenues. We should all be thinking more about production rather than distribution or sharing. I do not know of any country in the world that has developed just by its leaders gathering in their capital city every month to share revenues from rent.

During the 1994-95 Constitutional Conference, some of us argued that such organs as Federal Ministries of Education, Health, Agriculture and Sports were unnecessary. We reasoned that their responsibilities should be devolved to states and local governments. At best, the Federal Government should establish standards and regulatory bodies and give grants to states that conform to them. This proposal was not adopted by the constitutional conference, so the current structure was retained. Why should we be talking of federal roads and federal secondary schools? Decentralization is not an invitation to the breakup of the country and national unity should not continue to be confused with unitarism and concentration of power and resources at the federal level. Of course, I am aware that some of the main beneficiaries of our erstwhile regional parliamentary democracy have been hiding behind a call for restructuring to push for the breakup of the country because of their proximity to a finite natural resource and transient political power.

One of the consequences of excessive centralization and the military rule that facilitated it is that the Nigerian President is the most powerful president in the world. This is because he could quite literally unleash all security agencies on an individual or organization, undermine the National Assembly, and turn the judiciary into an almost pro-government and conformist organ. This is not in the realm of speculation; it has been happening in this country. Indeed, I drew attention to it when I was in office as vice president and was having a political face-off with my boss. It is not healthy for democracy and must be changed.

I also want to recall that during the said 1994-95 Constitutional Conference, Dr. Alex Ekwueme, GCON, the Second Republic vice president of this federation, introduced and canvassed for the concept of geo-political zones. I was among those who opposed it because I thought that Ekwueme, coming from the defunct Republic of Biafra, wanted to break up the country again. Now I realize that I should have supported him because our current federal structure is clearly not working. Dr. Ekwueme obviously saw what some of us, with our civil war mindset, could not see at the time. There is indeed too much concentration of power and resources at the centre. And it is stifling our march to true greatness as a nation and threatening our unity because of all the abuses, inefficiencies, corruption and reactive tensions that it has been generating.

There is need, therefore, to review the structure of the Nigerian federation, preferably along the basis of the current six geo-political zones as regions and the states as provinces. The existing states structure may not suffice, as the states are too weak materially and politically to provide what is needed for good governance.

In the same vein, I see nothing wrong with the establishment of state police by the states that want it, as long as it can be insulated from and is independent of the state or regional government. The argument that governors will abuse state police is rather specious. Should we abolish the Nigerian Police because it is often abused by those in power at the federal level? Should we abolish the state treasuries because governors abuse them? And should we also abolish local governments for the same reason? No. We should, as a people, struggle for and put in place institutional safeguards against abuse of power by those in power at all levels. We have a chance now to put many of those safeguards in a new constitution.

And, as is typical with working federations around the world, state flags or anthems should not get us overly excited. Local identities and symbols are not antithetical to and do not preclude national identities. I, for one, am a proud son of Adamawa, a proud Northerner and I am a proud citizen of Nigeria. American states all have flags and anthems; yet I do not know of many countries that are more stable and united than the United States of America.

It is also absurd to say that all parts of the country should have a uniform wage structure for workers. Our states and regions have different revenue endowments and varying costs of living. And it is misguided for labour leaders to think that a uniform wage structure across the country is in the best interest of workers. Employers, including state governments and agencies, that have the capacity to pay more should be able to do so. That can spur competition for the best talent, which may indeed raise overall wage levels (and standard of living) in the country. Minimum wage standards should, therefore, be established by state/regional governments.

Our judiciary is bloated, and increasingly conformist and pro-establishment. Yet justice is always delayed. In the US, which has a larger population and land mass, we find that the judiciary, while not bloated, delivers justice faster. I would like to see a more activist judiciary at all levels: local, regional and federal, one that does justice, rather than hide behind technicalities to do injustice. I would like to see a judiciary that is able to live up to its billing as the last hope of the common person.

On the specific theme of this conference (and without prejudice to the keynote address), I will just remark that I have long been an advocate of a two-party system because of our class, ethnic, religious and regional fault lines. My recommendation for legislative amendment in that regard is for the National Assembly to pass a law stating that there shall be two political parties in Nigeria, full stop. It does not have to decree their ideologies or platforms. This, in my view, will produce two political parties that will cut across our various divides, and be viable alternatives capable of forming government after elections. Ruling parties all over the world never want strong opposition parties and in contexts such as ours, are capable of undermining efforts by opposition parties to coalesce into a single formidable alternative party.

I thank the Leadership Newspapers group for organizing this event and for honouring me with the invitation to chair it. More importantly, I thank the newspaper for its commitment to the journalistic creed of holding those in power to account and reminding them and all of us that in a democracy, power flows or ought to flow from the people. I congratulate the recipients of today's awards.

Thank you and God bless.

Palace of the Sultan of Sokoto

"We must begin to think differently, Think big, and come out of our comfort zones. So the world would not continue to leave us behind."

Atiku Abubakar

4 THE REWARDS OF GIVING BACK

At the Inaugural D.M Ukpe Lecture celebrating the 35th Anniversary Homecoming of the Federal Government College, Okigwe Old Students' Association, Okigwe, Imo State, 17 November, 2012

I feel highly honoured and privileged to be invited to deliver the first D.M. Ukpe Lecture as part of this 35th anniversary homecoming of the Old Students' Association of the Federal Government College, Okigwe. I thank the association for this privilege and singular honour to be the Grand Patron of this vitally important association.

I thank the good people of Okigwe for hosting this Federal Government-owned institution and for the hospitality shown to its students and staff for these many years. I also thank them immensely for hosting us today. I also sincerely thank and congratulate Mr. D.M, Ukpe, who I am told, was the first principal of this school, and who, therefore, nurtured it from its infancy.

In a country where we rarely honour teachers for their critical contributions to societal development, it is praise-worthy that your former students and their friends and colleagues have decided to honour you in this enduring way. Thank you for your services to this school, this community and this country.
It is certainly good to be back in Imo State, among friends. And I am not really talking about political friends. Wherever people gather in this country in favour of education, they are my friends. Education is the best gift that we can give our children, the best legacy that we can leave for the next generation.
I shall be speaking on the rewards of giving back, which, I believe, fits very well with the theme of this homecoming: Mentoring as a Stimulus for Personal Growth and Organizational Development. Mentoring simply means guiding, teaching, advising and counselling someone, often a younger and/or less experienced person. It involves taking a person or some persons under your wings and helping to guide, teach and advise them with a view to helping them to become more successful in a given field or endeavour. Mentoring is critical for individuals, for organizations and for society. It ensures that a helping hand is extended to younger, less experienced persons or groups; it ensures leadership training and development, and a more successful transition to the next generation. It ensures that young people are equipped with the necessary cultural capital to assist them to navigate the complex world of education, work and even of politics.

Anyone who does not understand the power of mentoring only needs to look at the success of the Igbo in small (and not so small) businesses. I have no doubt that part of the factors that have ensured the relative sustenance of relative equality among the Igbo, even in the modern economy, is the apprenticeship system, otherwise known as the 'boy-boy' system. This is a system where small businessmen or tradesmen take young people (mostly boys), who may or may not be related to them and groom them in their business and in life, and, at the end of an agreed period of tutelage, give them some take-off capital to start their own business or trade. In return, of course, the apprentices provide a variety of services to their masters including helping in the business and domestic service. Call the 'boy-boy' system what you will (because of all its imperfections), but it is certainly also a mentoring system. And it has served the Igbo well, accounting for the wider spread of prosperity (or at least middle-class incomes) among this very industrious, resilient and adventurous group of Nigerians.

I am particularly delighted that the former students of this great school are pooling together to give back to their alma mater, and that you consider mentoring to be a critical ingredient in that effort. You are doing something very important. And it is something that you are not required to do. You are all volunteers, which makes your efforts much more remarkable and commendable. You are doing something that does not have an obvious material benefit to you. You could as well have moved on with your lives, without giving a damn about what goes on in your former school.

But there are rewards to giving back. Giving back is indeed a reward in itself. As humans, we are competitive beings; but we are also cooperative beings. Without cooperation, human society would be impossible. It is in our nature to look after each other, to give a helping hand to others even as we compete for scarce resources such as wealth, power and social honour and even sexual gratification. And there is the satisfaction derived from knowing that you can help and that you are helping other human beings. There is also the prestige of being associated with living, breathing, top quality schools such as: Barewa College; Government College, Keffi; Holy Ghost, Owerri; BSC, Orlu; DMGS, Onitsha; CIC, Enugu; Hope Waddell, Calabar; Kings' and Queens' Colleges, Lagos, to name just a few. Ever wondered why many Nigerians are quick to announce to you that they are alumni of Harvard University, even when all they did was attend a four-day course at that storied institution?

It is therefore important to help your alma mater reclaim its past glory and move it to greater heights. Your alma mater is a tag that you will continue to wear for as long as you are alive. Put another way, the reputation or notoriety of our alma mater follows us for the rest of our lives. Giving is good. When the Quran tells us that the hand of the giver is always on top, it is encouraging us to give.

And I do not think that there is a better way to give back than to help in the education of the young. When they say teach people how to fish rather than just give them fish, they are saying we should invest in education. When the Chinese say, "If it is for a lifetime educate the young", they are saying that education is the best investment we can make in society. Education is a vital vehicle for social advancement. It helps a society to bring up informed citizens who are more likely to know their rights and have a better appreciation for the rights of others. Education is a necessary ingredient for the exercise of freedom in modern societies. Education helps society develop its human resources and capacity. It helps to impart skills and knowledge necessary for people to better understand their surrounding environment and to apply such skills and knowledge in taking from as well as enriching and protecting that environment.

In the modern world, the countries that lead in education are also those that rank the best in other critical indices of development, including technological advancement, research, innovation and competitiveness, incomes, life expectancy, maternal health, and infant mortality. In well-run educational settings, ideas are freely exchanged, robust debates take place and received wisdoms challenged, validated or expunged - a process that is on-going and enduring and leads to improvements in the human condition. Conversely those corners of the world that reject education, demean it or fail to adequately invest in it, also tend to be the most backward corners of the world, lagging behind the rest in all measures of development and improvement of the human condition.

I think that giving back, especially through education, is something that every alumni association of our various schools should do: pool together and help your alma mater irrespective of government's investments and efforts in education or lack thereof. Giving back through education can take different forms: scholarships, books, laboratories, and other equipment and supplies, physical infrastructure such as classroom blocks, dormitories, bathrooms, mass transit vehicles, and mentorship, among other things. Education is a collective responsibility: we all benefited from public resources, whichever school we attended.

Those who do not belong to their alumni associations should join; and those who have not formed such associations should do so without delay. And it is not just about helping your old school; it is also about interacting with old school mates and friends, reminiscing about the past, reliving important moments and renewing shared values. Many societies have changed for the better because a group of school mates or classmates came together around common causes in the interest of their societies. They then worked together doggedly to realize their vision for their societies. Through the vehicle of your association, you can participate in and encourage mentorship, not only of the students and young graduates of your former school but across the country, including your places of work.

You can also as individuals and as a body lend your voices to the calls for the reform of our education and for increased public investment in education. However helpful they may be, alumni associations cannot substitute for governments in the development and promotion of public education. It remains primarily the responsibility of governments to make the necessary investments in education to ensure that citizens, whatever their state in life are afforded the opportunity to acquire an education. Therefore, we need, as a matter of urgency, major investments in public education. While the UNESCO recommendation of a quarter of the national budget may seem unrealistic for us now because of the crying need of other critical sectors, especially physical infrastructure and healthcare, it should be a goal of our governments. If we drastically reduce corruption and waste in the system, we can meet the UNESCO target. We cannot make the transition to a developed country if we do not develop our education and begin to produce those with the relevant skills and knowledge to build such an economy and society.

As some of you know, I am a founder of a private school system (from kindergarten to university levels) in Yola, in my home state of Adamawa. But I am a product of public education and would like every Nigerian child to have the same opportunities that I had to get good qualitative education. Private schools should just be supplements and niche players, rather than a replacement for good quality and accessible public education. I have to stress that strong, qualitative public education does not foreclose private education. The United States and United Kingdom are among the leading countries with strong public education and private education systems. The competition between private and public education is healthy for democracy.

Unfortunately, some people have resorted to blaming the growth of private education for the rot in the public education in Nigeria rather than see them as a response to the rot in the public school system. Some even call for taxes to be levied on private education. That would be a wrong-headed policy. We should strive to improve public education as a way to reduce the need for private education, or to make the latter a matter of choice rather than necessity for most parents and their wards. The growth of private education is not responsible for the rot in public education but it is rather a reaction to that rot, and a reflection of the lack of confidence in the governments to address it.

And we should not forget that private education has a long history in this country. The first schools in Nigeria, the mission schools, were private. And they coexisted with good quality public schools when governments started investing in education. There were also the various famous private schools such as Dr. Tai Solarin's Mayflower School, Ikenne, and Dr. B.U. Nzeribe's Santana schools in Awo-Omamma, here in Imo State. Oh, and by the way, the schools that Governor Rochas Okorocha built in four or so cities across the country have not prevented any government from improving public schools in those states.

Government control of schools or government monopoly of education in the Southern part of this country is a post-civil war phenomenon. It was part of the oil wealth-induced centralization and concentration of power in government. I am told that there was some punitive politics involved in the government take-over of schools in this part of the country. Whatever the case, while that action may have helped expand schooling and entrench secularism in our schools, the net effects have been largely negative. The schools declined in virtually every respect thus now having inadequate resources, facilities, qualified teachers, sanitation, and character-building, among other shameful inadequacies.

In addition to making the necessary investments in education, we must decentralize education and other sectors of our society. I will disappoint some of you, who are products of the so-called unity schools, the Federal Government Colleges. Consistent with my call for restructuring of the federation and devolution of powers to the constituent regions/states, I call on the Federal Government to hands off the direct control and administration of schools in the country. This should include 'unity schools'. The resources that go to them should be passed on to those states where they are located.

I know that some will say that the objective of promoting national unity will be compromised; others are likely to argue that their quality will further decline. I reject those arguments. They presuppose that the Federal Government has done a better job of managing resources and administering institutions in this country. That is questionable. Who would say that the University of Nigeria, Nsukka, University of Ife (now OAU), or Ahmadu Bello University Zaria were better run after they were taken over by the Federal Government than the regional governments that established them? Concentration of power and centralization of resources do not necessarily promote unity as Nigeria's case amply demonstrates.

And today we have a bizarre situation where states and even local communities on which federal universities are located, insist that the leaders of those universities must come from the locality. And they have largely been having their way. This completely negates the whole idea of university as an international centre of excellence, which should scour the world in search of the best talent to recruit as teachers and administrators. Some will say that the states are too poor to adequately resource these schools and other institutions. Again, that is a spurious argument. They are poor to the extent that the Federal Government is rich. The resources will have to be transferred to them as the responsibilities are. And the states, realizing that they can no longer blame the Federal Government for their own inadequacies, will sit up or be pressured by their people to do so. They will also sooner or later see the need to pool resources with their neighbouring states to provide infrastructure and services which would be more efficiently provided collaboratively. This will enable them to realize efficiencies and ensure more seamless service delivery. While public education is not for profit making, it will certainly benefit from such business principles as efficiency, accountability, and economies of scale.

When and if the Federal Government pulls out of building roads as I have advocated, and repatriates the funds to the states, what prevents Imo and Abia States from jointly rebuilding and dualizing the Owerri - Aba road or their portion of the Enugu - Port Harcourt highway? Why can't Imo, Abia and Anambra States, for instance, collapse the various public universities located in them into a single university system with multiple campuses and facilities with reduced administrative costs so that they spend more on the students' learning? To me, it can be done across the entire South-East geopolitical zone, and other zones in the country. We must begin to think differently, think big, and come out of our comfort zones so that the world would not continue to leave us behind.

Nigerians will know more about their country through education but more importantly through spatial mobility, commerce and justice. We must continue to promote freedom of movement and freedom of Nigerians to do business anywhere in the country. We must insist on unabbreviated citizenship whereby residency becomes the qualification for indigeneship rather than place of birth. We should be promoting healthy competition among the various states, zones and regions in the country to ensure a striving for excellence. In order to make all of these possible, we must make meaningful and urgent investments in the development of our infrastructure - roads, railways, air travel, and communication.

Think of the average Igbo man. He knows more about other parts of Nigeria through travel and sojourn in those other parts of the country. So, let us build roads and railways across the length and breadth of this country; let us build and better equip our airports and improve air travel; let us build more schools all over Nigeria and let people travel freely and safely and engage in commerce and other legitimate activities. When we can move more freely and reside and do business wherever we want, our children will also attend schools in various parts of the country, thereby coming in contact with those from other parts of the country. And they will learn more about and become indigenes of those other parts. That interaction, the sense of freedom and the sense of justice that would result from all of these, will more likely make us more united as a people and more committed to the success and security of our country.

Thank you and God bless.

Aboko Boat Regatta, Kogi State

ATA GALA

"This balance between the National and State governments ought to be dwelt on with peculiar attention, as it is of the utmost importance. It forms a double security to the people. If one encroaches on their rights, they will find a powerful protection in the other. Indeed, they will both be prevented from overpassing their constitutional limits by a certain rivalship, which will ever subsist between them."

Alexander Hamilton

5 FEDERALISM AND INTER-GOVERNMENTAL RELATIONS

At the book launch in honour of Alhaji (Dr.) Bamanga M. Tukur CON, Abuja, 22 November, 2012

I am delighted to be present at the launch of this book in honour of my brother, my party leader and one of Nigeria's most eminent personalities, Alhaji (Dr.) Bamanga Tukur, CON.

I commend the book's author, Oluseyi Adetanmi, for the work put into the book and for honouring the Tafida Adamawa and Wakilin Ganye with its publication.

Certainly, a book that deals with federalism and inter-governmental relations in Nigeria is quite timely. In recent times, a good number of Nigerians have been seized with debates and contestations about the nature of our federalism and the appropriate relations between the central government and the constituent parts of our country - states, local government and even geo-political zones. Related to those are the questions around revenue and power sharing among these constituent jurisdictions.

While the questions of power and revenue sharing between the centre and the constituent units, and among the constituent units are legal questions, they are also profoundly political questions. Political struggles and agreements lead to legal codifications. And each legal codification produces winners and losers and can lead to new political questions, which may yet lead to changes in the law to account for new realities and balance of political forces.

Human societies are dynamic, and political actors are key drivers of that dynamism. We must continue to debate our present and our future. Nothing in the affairs of nations is cast in stone. We must continue to renew our federalism. We must continue to reflect on the structure of our relationships to see whether we are served better by existing structures or whether those need tinkering with or transforming fundamentally.

Let us not forget that there was a time when the regions of this country were truly powerful and handled their affairs just fine. Our schools were of better quality then, our graduates were of better quality then; we adapted education to local needs; and we built and maintained our roads and bridges. We paid attention to a variety of economic activities that provided jobs and raised government revenue. And there was little oil revenue to share then. The addiction to oil revenues seems to have dulled our senses. It seems to be making us not only to ignore other sectors of the economy but more importantly, to resist the urgent need to renew our federalism to be better able to face the challenges of this century. The excessive centralization which began with military rule, with the pretext of promoting national unity, seems clearly to be undermining our unity as a nation. It has increasingly robbed constituent states of autonomy and resources to plan and implement development projects in ways that address local needs and priorities. This unfortunate situation needs to change and change quickly.

The ongoing debate on the structure of our federation is healthy. I believe that we need to devolve more powers to the constituent elements of our federation and re-allocate revenues to match the devolution. The fear that local leaders, such as governors, will become too powerful is not a good reason for us not to do the right thing. We cannot let timidity prevent us from renewing our federation. All politics are local. Our people have the capacity to ask the right questions and make the right demands of their local leaders. And they have the capacity to struggle to realize those demands. They will pressure their local leaders, including governors, to fulfil their responsibilities or be voted out of office. The impunity that we have experienced in the hands of some elected power wielders in the last 13 years or so of democracy will continue to be challenged; and the local level, being closer to the people, is the easier site at which to struggle for and achieve the desired results. That should be our focus as we try to deepen our democracy and give our people the reasons to support and celebrate that democracy.

Thank you and God bless.

Ijele Masquerade

"Education should be the responsibility of state/regional and local governments the Federal Government should, at best, set standards and provide financial support for states that follow them."

Atiku Abubakar

6 REDISCOVERING THE NIGERIAN LOCAL GOVERNMENT SYSTEM IN THE EMERGING CONSTITUTION

At the National Conference organized by the Association of Local Governments of Nigeria, Enugu, 28 November, 2012

I am very pleased and honoured to be invited to this National Conference on Rediscovering the Nigerian Local Government System in the Emerging Constitution. I thank the organizers of this conference and the leadership of ALGON for inviting me and for selecting this very important theme.

I am reminded that this is also the 13th anniversary of the formation of ALGON. That anniversary does bring back good memories to me. I recall playing a role, as the then vice president, in the formation of this association. In fact, I was among those who actively encouraged its formation. I did so because of my deep belief in the viability, importance and effectiveness of local administration. I also believed then and still believe now, that local leaders across the country needed to have a forum for interaction, for exchange of ideas and for the promotion of healthy rivalry to spur development and best practices in administration and management. I also thought that our local leaders needed a strong collective voice for constructive intervention in national decision making relating to local administration and other related matters.

In fact, I recall that when I inaugurated ALGON on 30th November, 1999 at the African Women Centre, Abuja, the main objectives of forming the association were listed as, among other things, the promotion and protection of the rights, privileges, interests and autonomy of Local Governments for the ultimate survival of the local government councils in Nigeria.

I am glad that many of those objectives have been realized and that you have sustained the spirit and momentum. I heartily congratulate you.

But clearly challenges remain. There is still a lot of work to be done. There are still objectives to be met and goals to attain. An issue at the forefront of current discussions on constitution amendment is the autonomy of local governments. Nigeria's local governments still lack reasonable autonomy to provide services and implement development projects for the local populations in an efficient and timely manner. Taking a cue from the overbearing Federal Government, state governments have been overbearing in their relationship with local administrations. Many have been abusing the joint State-Local Government accounts by tampering with local government funds, as reports and petitions make clear. Interestingly, while these abuses go on, many local government leaders are unable to say so for fear of angering their state governments.

The direct allocation of funds from the federation account to local governments was meant to ensure that the local governments get development funds from the centre to enhance their operational capacity. At the same time, the joint State/LG account was meant to acknowledge the rightful role of the federating states in local government administration. However, the control that the state governments have over the joint account has ensured that the development objective of the direct allocation is not met. And it has left the local governments worse off than they were prior to that policy shift.

While most agree that this is a problem, there is a divergence of opinions on what the proper relationship between the three tiers of government should be. The most popular seems to be the call for constitutional amendment to guarantee local government autonomy, especially on the question of the joint account with state governments. The claim here is that the abolition of the joint account would ensure that governors will not tamper with local government funds. However popular that may seem at the moment, it may not be a very smart idea going forward. The temptation to enshrine in the constitution the nature of the relationship between the three tiers of government, especially in a manner that seeks to sidestep the state governments, may lead to more problems for local administration than seems apparent now.

I believe that we need to re-examine our conception of local government administration. Should we continue with the practice of the Federal Government creating local governments across the country and allocating resources to them directly? Or should it be left in the hands of federating states to decide for themselves the system of local government and the number of local authorities they need because of our historical and cultural differences?

In my view, there are three critical issues here. First is the structure of our federation; the second is our political practice; and the third is our disregard for rules and regulations. In a federation, local administration ought to be left in the hands of federating states or regions rather than an awkward situation where the local governments deal directly with the Federal Government while side-tracking the state governments. The federating units should be left to determine the system and number of local governments and fund them accordingly in accordance with their historical and cultural peculiarities and development needs.

Our focus should be on ensuring a more effective local administration, responsible fiscal management and accountability. And the proximity of state governments to local governments makes them more suited for that than the more distant Federal Government. All politics is local. The Federal Government lacks the capacity to monitor every local level development or issue in this country. For instance, the Federal Government has little inclination or resources to find out whether the Adamawa State government is fulfilling its obligations to Ganye Local Government, and to hold the state government to account. The Federal Government is simply too distant to monitor what happens at that local level. It is for the people of Ganye Local Government and those of other local governments to hold the state government to account. And in a federal system, it is in our collective interest to strengthen the local level.

On the question of political practice, for as long as our politics remains the domain of controlling godfathers at the federal and state levels devoid of internal party democracy, so long will our local governments remain at the beck and call of whoever chooses contestants for local electoral offices. The point is that even if local government funds come directly from the Federal Government and without the mediation of joint state-local government accounts, the dominant role of governors, rather than party members, in selecting candidates for local electoral offices, would still not ensure autonomous, effective and responsive local government administration. Therefore, we need to find ways to ensure internal party democracy so that the selection of candidates for elections to the local and other levels is carried out by the generality of party members rather than a few godfathers. At the local government level, we should indeed allow independent candidature.

My dear friends, the central government did not create local governments prior to military rule and you will agree with me that we had a more effective and responsive local government administration then. The Federal Government started creating local governments across the country at the same time that we lost our heads to oil revenue. Thus, local governments have become even more dependent on the Federal Government than the state governments. That is an anomaly.

It is our over-centralization of power and excessive concentration of resources at the federal level and the abandonment of due process and regulations under military rule that led to the state governments' abuse of local administrations. That is what led to the pressure for direct federal allocation to local governments and its subsequent provision in our current constitution. If we amend our constitution to have a genuine federal system rather than the near unitary system that we currently have, then there would be no need for statutorily mandated direct federal allocation to local governments. There would be no need to enshrine the number of local governments in the constitution. Other than direct fiscal allocation to local governments, what other rationale exists for enshrining the number of local governments in the constitution and making the creation of additional ones virtually impossible for state governments? What if a local government such as the one that is hosting us today experiences rapid growth in population and, for administrative convenience and effectiveness, the state government wishes to split it into two or more local governments? Why should such a split be made very difficult for the state? I believe that the federal share of national revenues should be whittled down while the allocation to states should be increased, including the funds hitherto going directly to local governments from the centre.

Ladies and gentlemen, all over the world, serious governments tax their citizens and corporations to raise revenues for development purposes and service delivery. For that reason, governments work hard to promote economic development, to create a strong tax base. That is what we did prior to military rule and prior to oil's significant contributions to our national revenues. That is what makes people hold their governments to account. Currently, however, our local governments, like the state governments, look up to Abuja for monthly revenue allocations. That kind of dependence does not make for any meaningful autonomy, and it sure will not bring about meaningful development.

Every tier of government should be reasonably self-reliant in terms of revenues. The revenues that it gets from the other tier(s) should only be supplementary otherwise it will lack a reasonable degree of autonomy, irrespective of what the laws say. That is the reality of the human condition and of politics. And that is why I have been calling for the devolution of more powers and revenues from the Federal Government to the state/regional governments. It is not political posturing; it is a critical condition for the deepening of our democracy and promoting national development, peace and security.

As you deliberate, you may also wish to consider what would be the best institutional arrangements for managing inter-governmental relations; the codification of the procedures for election, functions, removal from office and the appointment of the key local government officers; the administration of the Federal Capital Territory and designated federal areas; and, above all, how to democratize our political parties.

I wish you successful deliberations.

Thank you and God bless.

Sabuwar Kofa, Kano City Gate

"Education is the most powerful weapon which you can use to change the world."

Nelson Mandela

7 REBUILDING PUBLIC EDUCATION AS A BRIDGE TO NIGERIA'S FUTURE

At the 2012 Shehu Musa Yar'Adua Memorial Lecture, Abuja, 8 December, 2012

I hesitated when I was asked by the Yar'Adua Foundation to give the Yar'Adua Memorial lecture for this year. I was the Tafida's close friend and political protégé, and so I felt that I would be a biased speaker. I thought that it would be better to continue with our tradition of bringing in world figures to speak at these events. However, when I was told that I would be speaking on education as a bridge to Nigeria's future, I dropped my earlier hesitation. I am certainly not an expert in the field of education, but I believe that I could add my voice to the calls for a major review of our educational policies and institutions to properly position this country for the challenges of development.

The Tafida loved education and appreciated its value in society's improvement. Nobody remembers this better than his wife, Hajia Binta Yar'Adua, who said, with respect to the scholarship programme established in the Tafida's name by this Foundation: "Shehu and I shared a belief that education is the bedrock of an enlightened society where all Nigerians, regardless of their status or background, are able to participate in the development of the nation." That scholarship, the Yar'Adua Merit Scholars Programme, is meant to cultivate the talents and abilities of this nation's children. And the Tafida clearly understood the vital links among education and infrastructural provisioning, social welfare and the environmental protection for the development of a nation. At his Presidential Campaign Declaration on February 25, 1992, he stated, "Our defined national purpose must seek to correct the present tendency to segment rather than integrate the various sectors of our national life." Thus, he called for investments in healthcare, education and training, housing, infrastructure, social welfare, environmental protection, among other things. He also called for an overhaul of our policy making and the policy environment to meet those challenges.

Why Education?

Like the late Tafida, I believe strongly in the power of education and its strategic value in the transformation of a nation and its peoples. And for me, it is also personal. My father was once imprisoned for not letting me go to school. While sending him to prison may have been harsh then, denying me an education would have turned out to be a harsher punishment. Education gave me a career in the civil service; it helped me succeed in business and helped me to make the modest achievements that I have made in politics. And, above all, it gave me a global outlook on life. In short, education gave me what I have today.

Education is a critical path for social advancement. It helps a society to bring up informed citizens who are more likely to know their rights and have a better appreciation for the rights of others. The exercise of freedom in the modern world requires education. Education helps society develop its human resources and capacity. It helps to impart the skills and knowledge, necessary for the individual to better understand the surrounding environment and to apply such skills and knowledge in taking from, as well as enriching and protecting that environment. It is obvious that the countries that lead in education today are also those that rank the best in other critical indices of development, including technological advancement, research, innovation and competitiveness, economic growth and diversification, incomes, health, life expectancy, infant mortality, and maternal health, in properly run educational settings, ideas are freely exchanged, robust debates take place and received wisdoms challenged, validated or expunged - a process that is on-going and enduring and leads to improvements in the human condition.

Of course, Western education brings with it ideas and practices that challenge some traditional beliefs and practices, which is part of why it is sometimes resisted. But the real question on that score is whether we would be better off without Western education or not. The answer is pretty obvious: No.

The Context

Western style education was formally introduced in Nigeria in 1845, with the establishment of the first primary school in Badagry, which enrolled 40 students. Since then, and particularly after our independence in 1960, Western education, despite initial (and even current) resistance in some quarters, has grown in Nigeria. And it has made enormous contributions to the country and its peoples. At the time of independence in 1960, school enrolment figures were 2.9 million, 135,000, and 4,000 for primary, secondary and tertiary schools respectively. By 2009, (the last year for which data are available) the figures had risen to 24 million, 5 million, and 1.5 million respectively. If you add the over 1 million registered in UME in 2009, the figure for tertiary education for that year would be 2.7 million. These figures clearly show that there has been enormous expansion in our education in terms of enrolment. The number of schools has also expanded enormously as has the cost to the public purse.

Yet, we are aware that too many of our sons and daughters, who ought to be in school or who desire to be in school are not in school. Data from a recent UNESCO study indicate that Nigeria has 10.5 million children who are not in school, the worst of such case in the world. And we have too many uneducated adults among us, whose lives would likely have been better with education. The figures vary across the country with my home zone of the North East faring the worst. So, we have a dire need for the expansion of school spaces across the country.

In addition to the issue of quantity, there is the question of quality. It is true that every generation tends to think that the quality of education was better during its time, but the Nigerian case is clearly besides that point. Employers of labour, including public and private sector employers, lament the poor quality of graduates and other school leavers in this country. Many of our schools are unable to meet the minimum standards for accreditation of their programs as set by the relevant regulatory agencies, and in recent times, some international regulatory agencies have started to reject graduates of some programs in some of our erstwhile premier universities.

The WAEC and NECO results for many years now clearly show that our secondary schools are not adequately helping our students become the best that they can be. Our primary schools are obviously not better with many pupils learning under very harsh conditions and environment. Many of our young people are roaming the streets of our major cities, either begging or engaging in the marginal hawking of products with little income to justify the risks to them and the nuisance to society. And we have thousands of university graduates who remain unemployed or underemployed, despite the enormous resources put in by their families and the government for their education. The International Labour Organization estimates the number of our unemployed young people to be 75 million this year.

Ironically, we also have thousands of jobs available in certain sectors such as information and communications technology, which cannot be filled because of the scarcity of requisite skills in the available graduates. Enrolment and admissions have not kept up with our population growth, and quality, rather than keep pace with our needs, has deteriorated a great deal, making our degrees increasingly worthless. Many private schools have emerged to fill some of the void but they are still inadequate and some of them are also of questionable quality. They too need to be properly regulated by professionals to ensure that quality is maintained.

I need to note here that the crisis in our educational system is not an isolated one. It is instead an extension of, a cause of and a consequence of the general crisis of governance and development in the country. The poor planning that characterizes our educational system is a reflection of the poor planning and execution that characterize governance in the country. The corruption, which seems to have become endemic in our schools, is a reflection of the corruption in the society and in our governance structures. The impunity and dictatorial tendencies of some educational administrators and teachers also reflect the dominance of such tendencies in the wider society, especially in institutions of government. And these have been around for a long time.

Propositions

While these problems are severe and urgent, I submit that we proceed to solve them in a very methodical, deliberate and sustainable way. I propose that we should seek not just to solve the problems for today, but do so with our eyes also trained on the future. We must not adopt our usual fire brigade approach. Therefore, we must change the way we formulate policies on education. In that regard, I hereby make a few modest proposals which, if adopted, will help us to begin to dig ourselves out of the deep hole that our educational system has fallen. And our people, especially our young people and our country generally will benefit from them.

1. **Informed Discussion:** We need an informed national discussion on what we want out of our education. What should we expect of our schools? What are our priorities? Shouldn't we follow the more serious countries as they try to emphasize math and reading in their school reforms, to be able to compete in the modern technology-driven global economy? Should we emphasize the current homogenous educational system that treats all students as though they have the same capacity and are headed in the same academic and career direction?

Or should we instead revert to the model that hitherto existed in many parts of the country, whereby students are streamed into different tracks depending on their proven abilities, interests and aptitudes? In the latter case, some students would proceed to universities and polytechnics, while some would proceed to technical schools and other specialized institutes where they learn relevant trades such as carpentry, bricklaying, welding, and farming. I believe that the latter model will not only help school leavers find immediate employment, but also help to elevate the knowledge base and quality of trades-people and farmers in the country.

2. **Policy Process:** We need a policy process in education. We need to clearly identify and regularly follow a set of clear principles and steps in the formulation of educational policy. The long years of military and quasi-military rule in Nigeria have led to the abandonment of process and procedures in the formulation of educational and other development policies in Nigeria. These days what typically happens is that a minister, commissioner or head of a department or agency gets a brain wave, puts together a memo to the appointing authority and gets an approval for the implementation of major policies that have serious implications for the country or a section thereof. To be fair, the fellow may have only good intentions, but good intentions are certainly not enough. Major policy shifts need to go through proper review by experts and subjected to public discussion to ascertain their merits and demerits and explore the various implications of such policy shifts.

3. **Planning:** Related to the question of policy process is the near absence of planning in current development efforts in Nigeria. When a decision is finally made to adopt an educational policy or programme, we must plan properly for its implementation. Education is for a lifetime and, therefore, we must never be in an undue haste to implement half-baked, ill-thought-out policies. We must never grope our way through implementation. When was the last time that we had a proper national discussion and debate on the future direction of our education with structured efforts to gather inputs from various stakeholders including teachers, students, parents, educational administrators, employer groups, government agencies and donors? We should take deliberate steps to plan and in doing so we must take the long view but with built-in flexibility to adapt to rapid changes in society such as in the economy, politics, demography and security. And planning requires reliable data.

It is a shame that we have managed to make a mess of virtually every census in this country for what we think to be political advantage. But it has grave implications for planning. How can we plan properly for education when we only possess a vague idea of how many children of school age we have or will have in the next few years? How can we plan when we do not even know the number of students in secondary schools in a particular state or how many teachers we have or will need and what the training needs are and/or will be in the next five years?

We must remember that each time we play politics with counting or allow corruption to prevent accurate counting in schools, we are implicitly taking steps to prevent proper planning for the improvement of our people's lives. As we work out our census headaches, we should at least allow the compulsory registration of births and deaths in the country to assist in planning for the next generation.

4. **Professionalism:** We need professionalism in the planning and implementation of educational policies. Politicians and political leaders in government can articulate policy goals and directions, but the planning and implementation of educational policy and programs should be left in the hands of professionals. And they should get the necessary support and resources to do the job well for the interest of the country or the specific part.

5. **Decentralization:** Education should be the responsibility of state/regional and local governments. The Federal Government should, at best, set standards and provide financial support for states that follow them. We do not need a federal ministry of education that is burdened with running secondary and tertiary institutions across the country. If we must have one, it should focus on establishing standards and enforcing them with incentives and sanctions. State/regional governments should have the freedom to plan and implement educational policies and programmes to suit local needs and changing circumstances.

   While a university in the Niger Delta or Lagos may see an urgency in having a world class maritime program, one in Yola or Bauchi may prioritize information technology or agriculture while yet another in Jos or Enugu may prioritize Geology or Metallurgy. Whatever the case, it should be for local political, bureaucratic, business and educational leaders to make such informed decisions. A healthy competition in the field of education among our various states and localities will be a boon for Nigeria's development. And they are more likely to quickly adapt their educational processes and programs to suit changing local needs, within the context of the dynamic national and global economy.

6. **Autonomy of School Boards and University Councils:** To ensure the ability of schools to quickly meet their challenges, we must restore autonomy to local school boards, and the councils and senates of tertiary educational institutions. Over the years, the excessive centralization of power and resources in the Federal Government has been replicated in the states such that school leaders do not have much power in policy making and execution. And the little power that they have, they have exercised as though they are sole administrators.

   So long as they stay in the good book of National Universities Commission, like the president or governor, they pretty much do whatever they like. And these political leaders do not always have the correct or complete information to make informed decisions about the goings-on in these schools. This authoritarianism breeds corruption and resistance and conflict in these schools as is evident in the numerous petitions government agencies receive on the school leaders as well as the countless paid advertisements and sponsored write-ups in our newspapers and magazines.

The recent report of the Kano State governor appointing the principal officers of the new state university reflects the existing practice across the country. This must change. Collegiality, probity, due process and accountability must be restored to our educational system. The recent reports that the security agencies would now be monitoring the distribution of books across the country by the Universal Basic Education Commission because of the diversion of some of those books to private ends illustrates my point. We do not need that kind of centralization. Besides, a child in a primary school in Yola does not have to read the same books as the one in Ikeja or Kalahari.

7. **Agility and Flexibility:** Public schools should be nimble enough and autonomous enough and equipped adequately to compete with private schools. The latter should not be the public's only choice for good quality education, but an alternative for those who choose to. While public schools are not profit-making organizations, and should not be, they will be run better with some business principles such as efficiency, merit, reward for hard work, and innovation, among other factors. And, working with government, the organized private sector and professional groups, they will be able to quickly adapt to changing economic conditions and national priorities to create programs that produce graduates with relevant skills for immediate employment.

8. **Free and Compulsory Primary and Secondary Education:** I call for the institution of free and compulsory primary and secondary education across the country, with federal support for states that agree to abide by them and meet set standards.

   We should in fact have a law that mandates anyone one under the age of 18 to be in school and hold parents accountable for non-compliance. This will ensure that most of our citizens complete secondary school education. But it should not be implemented the way we typically go about these things. A target date should be set to allow for data collection and proper planning. We need to know the impact that such a policy will have for enrolment, school space and other resources, number of teachers, their availability and training, the impact on the demand for tertiary education and the cost of all of these.

   We should then have a system in place that provides adult education for those who missed the boat in the past but would like to get an education. This is what serious countries do in order to lift most of their citizens and provide the needed human resources for their economic, social and political development. We should then allow fees to rise slowly in the tertiary institutions to help pay for the badly needed improvements in infrastructure and quality.

9. **Teacher Recruitment, Training, Reward and Evaluation:** Anyone who has passed through our educational system will agree with me that we have many bad teachers as we have bad politicians and other professionals. We cannot truly transform teaching and learning unless we encourage the recruitment, training and retraining

of excellent teachers, improved reward for those who excel and easing out of those who fail to improve. We must make teaching an attractive profession, rather than one that people go into when they cannot find a better paying, better resourced and better regarded profession. I would like to see a situation where our schools compete with the banks, oil companies and telecommunications companies, among others, for the best talent in the country and around the world. We cannot get to that point unless we make the necessary investments in education that prioritise teacher training, recruitment, a merit-based reward system that compare with other highly rewarded professions, and an accountability system to match.

Investment in teachers is an investment in students, in education, and therefore, in our future. We should not merely continue to rely on WAEC and NECO results to tell us how well or badly our students are doing. We need to put in place systems for gathering data on student performance, graduation, dropout rates, and tertiary education success. This will help us to hold schools, teachers and administrators accountable for what happens to their students.

10. **Centres of Excellence:** Serious countries also have centres of excellence among public institutions of secondary and higher learning: the think houses and research leaders. Such centres attract the best and brightest among teachers, researchers and students, who desire to go there and participate in cutting-edge academic and research pursuits. And they are deliberately well-resourced to induce the kind of environment needed to nurture exceptional talent. Their impact on the overall quality of education and innovation in society are enormous.

My dear friends, one of the possible advantages of coming late to the technological age (if we can call it that), is that a country can leap-frog certain stages that the early arrivals or adopters went through. As we made a technological leap to wireless phones and wireless Internet, we can also leap to high-paying jobs for our people, if we make the right investments in infrastructure, education and innovation right now. Such investments will attract cutting-edge world class companies to invest in Nigeria and make our labour force globally mobile and highly rewarded. Recently, the US Secretary of Education, Arne Duncan, told his compatriots, "We have to educate our way to a better economy... The path to the middle class today runs straight through the classroom." If this is true for the leading country in the world, it is certainly truer for our rather backward country, Nigeria.

Mr. Chairman, ladies and gentlemen, I have deliberately failed to emphasize the issue of adequate funding for our education. This is partly because all too often we seem to believe that throwing money at problems will somehow magically solve them. But problems that are widespread and which have festered for a very long time cannot be solved simply by throwing money at them. Americans call such a thoughtless practice "throwing good money after bad". We must make the structural, institutional and policy changes that are crying out for attention. As we do those and engage in proper planning, we shall have a better sense of the resources that are needed for our educational rebirth - what we can afford and the best way to deploy them - as a country, state or locality. In any case, I believe that if we reduce corruption and waste in our system, we will be able to allocate a quarter of our budgets to education, in line with the recommendation of UNESCO. And it will be a sound investment to make.

Ladies and gentlemen, I readily acknowledge that education will not solve all our developmental problems; but we really can't solve them without transforming and improving our education. And doing so will be a very good way to honour the memory of my friend, mentor and a great Nigerian, the late Shehu Musa Yar'Adua, the Tafida of Katsina.

Thank you and God bless.

Tafawa Balewa Square, Lagos

"There are forces all around you who wish to exploit division,
Rob you of your freedom, And tell you what to think. But young
folks can rekindle the weary spirit of a slumbering nation."

Wynton Marsalis

8 EDUCATION, GOOD GOVERNANCE AND NATIONAL UNITY

At the Unity Schools Old Students' Association One-Day Summit/Dialogue on Education Good Governance & National Unity, Abuja, 24 October 2013

I am delighted to be here among all of you, who are gathered here because you care about education. In the midst of the continuing crisis in our educational system, including the on-going strike by university teachers, which has led to the closure of our public universities for four months, it is commendable that the alumni of our unity schools are organizing this summit. I derive special pleasure when I am among those who spare a thought for our education and organize to find ways to improve education in our country.

Education is the key to our future, not oil, not solid minerals. For us to rapidly develop this country and improve the living standards of our people, we must focus on human capital development, i.e. education. And it cannot be achieved through business as usual in our educational system. We need to rethink what we are doing in and with education. The world is leaving us behind so we need to act fast.

I, therefore, hope that this summit will deliberate on the future of our education generally, including unity schools. In my view, some of the issues that need to be considered include the structure of ownership and funding of our public schools, whether we should focus on numerical increases of our schools or consider merging and growing the existing schools, the use of modern technology such as computers, e-books and e-libraries to improve teaching and learning and to reduce cost. We also need to consider the role of education in citizen enlightenment, skills acquisition and economic development, as well as what curriculum reviews or modifications will follow from those considerations. And as we do these we should endeavour to follow international best practices because our country, our students and our businesses will have to compete and win in that international arena.

On unity schools specifically, I am on record as an advocate of greater devolution of powers in this country. I firmly believe that education should be the responsibility of state and local governments, with the Federal Government setting standards and ensuring their enforcement. But if the Federal Government Colleges must remain federally owned, then we must quickly reverse the trend towards their localization. We must go back to the vision and mission of the unity schools: move students and teachers of the unity schools outside their region to foster brotherhood and nationhood. And we need that now more than ever before.

I commend the Unity Schools' Old Students' Association for its efforts in organizing the alumni of the Federal Government Colleges and for organizing this summit. There is an urgent need for the formation of and alumni development across all schools in Nigeria. I call on Nigerians to join the alumni of their alma mater and to form alumni associations of their former schools, if they do not already exist. Anybody who attended public schools in Nigeria benefitted from the country and its people, and I believe that most would like to give back to the country. However, we need to find the time and ways to ask them.

One of my aides, who has degrees from two Nigerian universities and a degree from one foreign university once told me how the alumni association and development office of the foreign university in question has followed him around the world in the different countries and institutions that he has worked in, updating him on developments in the university and soliciting his support. But none of the Nigerian universities that he attended has ever contacted him. At the minimum, this tells us how far we need to go in developing alumni associations and getting them to help the schools that helped to nurture them and contribute to their success.

While government remains and should be the most important organ for the development of education, we, as citizens, and corporate organizations have to contribute in the many ways that we can, to help build our education to meet the challenges of the 21st century. Once more, I thank the organizers for inviting me, and I thank you for your attention.

Abuja, 24 October, 2013

buja Ecumenical Church

"The excessive dominance of the Federal Government has been detrimental to the development aspirations of all sections of this country."

Atiku Abubakar

9 MEDIA, YOUTH AND NIGERIA'S DEVELOPMENT CHALLENGES

At the Conference of the African Council for Communication Education, University of Nigeria, Nsukka, 10 March, 2014

I understand that this is a conference that brings together communication educators across Africa. I have, however, chosen to focus my lecture mainly on Nigeria for the simple reason that I think Nigeria must hurry to put its house in order so that it can live up to its responsibility to help Africa put its house in order. If Nigeria gets its right, much of Africa will get it right.

It feels good to once more visit the University of Nigeria, Nsukka. I must confess that whenever I step into UNN or Ahmadu Bello University or Obafemi Awolowo University (formerly UNIFE), I have mixed feelings. Such a visit brings back memories of when Nigeria and Nigerians were on the road to greatness, with all our imperfections. But it also brings forth to me what has gone wrong in and with our country and our people. When I talk about what has gone wrong, I am not just talking about the broken infrastructure in our universities, the lecturers that have fled the country, the empty libraries with outdated books and journals or rotten hostels that are not good enough to be prison cells but in which young adults are crammed and are expected to learn. I am not talking about the 'sorting' (favours for grades) that is said to be widespread. Those are certainly important.

Rather, I am talking about how we seem to have lost sight of what federating units and local peoples are able to achieve when they have the autonomy to look after themselves rather than being spoon-fed from the national capital. I am also talking about how we seem to be forgetting what selfless public service means: not one of those three universities that I just mentioned was built or owned by the federal government in the First Republic. They were built by the regional governments largely from their resources. And one more thing: not one of the leaders who conceived of and built these universities, namely Dr. Nnamdi Azikiwe, Sir Ahmadu Bello and Chief Obafemi Awolowo, seriously considered locating them in their villages. Rather, they chose places where they thought would be best suited for such ivory towers and the work done in them and the role they play in society.

Those were strong federating units but today, we have severely weakened states nearly totally dependent on fiscal allocations from Abuja. I have not come across a serious country that has developed in that way.

Today, we have federal ownership of universities and other institutions and the clamour for even more federal takeover of more establishments. Today, we have leaders insisting on locating public universities in their villages or relocating existing ones there. Today, we have people, including intellectuals, insisting that the leaders of universities and even the lecturers must come from the states where they are located. This is the kind of negative messaging that we have been exposing our youth to in recent times. And it must stop if we are to be taken seriously in the comity of nations and in the world's intellectual circles. Universities ought to be international centres of excellence rather than mediocre enclaves of local champions.

I founded a university with the help of some of my friends. The mandate given to the university by the Board of Trustees, under my guidance, is to scout the world for the best professors and administrators that can be attracted to Yola to work at the university. We are attempting to build a world class university, not a Yola or Adamawa or even a Nigerian champion. That is my understanding of a university.

As it is with universities, so it is with countries. If we want to build world class countries we must do things differently and the media have a critical role to play in that regard.
What should such a role be? What should be the role of the media in national development; in the empowerment of our youth and children? What kind of messaging from the media can help accomplish those?

Put differently, how can the media help to advance the interests of our youth and children in the effort at national rebirth or transformation? How can they help our youth to help themselves and our nation? How can the media help us build an economy for the future that empowers and protects our youth? How can the youth take advantage of opportunities and help transform themselves and the country?

I am not an expert on media and youth but I do know a thing or two about helping young people to learn and putting them to work. I am sure that this conference will deliberate a great deal on the role of the media in our society, especially its role in the lives of our youth and children.

The role of the media in communications, in entertainment, in education and in mobilization carries with it enormous responsibilities. The mass media do not just communicate content, they create content as well. The media often sets the agenda for debate, structure the discourse and set the tone (sometimes with help from politicians, of course). This is an enormous amount of power that must be exercised responsibly, especially in a young and emerging democracy such as ours.
We often charge the mass media with promoting national development and national unity, and with protecting our youth. That is fine, but as a nation and a people, we need some understanding of and consensus around what must be done to improve the country and the youth before we can realistically charge the media with promoting them. From my interactions with ordinary Nigerians, and my experience in business and government and my travels, I have come to understand that a few priority areas stand out and must quickly be addressed in order for our people and our country to realize our full potentials and help our youth and children realize their dreams. These are the provision of and access to high quality education and training; infrastructure such as power, roads, railways and ports; security; anti-corruption and accountability, employment and job creation. There is also the issue of reorientation of values, which, I think, will come more from the change of behaviour by leaders than from mere talk.

And at this time that Nigeria's national unity is under stress, leaders and the media must help to keep us together not by mouthing tired clichés about our indivisibility but by doing the hard work of acknowledging and managing our differences in ways that bring out the best in all of us as a collective entity. We must play to our strengths as a diverse country, respect our diversity and varying levels of development, allow the federating states the autonomy to develop at their respective paces and to address their peculiar needs and challenges.

Ladies and gentlemen, we cannot do the same thing over and over and expect a different outcome. We must not only learn from our past but from practices that work well in different parts of the world, to help our people and our country to transition to a nation that is able to care for its people.

Let me just focus on education in Nigeria as an example. We cannot significantly improve education in this country, if we continue with the current overly centralized system with suffocating federal control. Federal schools should be handed over to the states in which they are located and the budgetary resources hitherto expended on them transferred to those state governments. The Federal Government should focus on setting up regulatory standards and enforcing those standards. It will be easier for authorities at the UNN to show the officials in Enugu what life at UNN is really like than officials in Abuja. And it will be easier for those officials at Enugu to hold the leaders of UNN accountable. It will also be easier for the students and the UNN community to demand accountability from their school leaders as they too can easily reach the officials at Enugu. Beyond mere distance and the streamlining of authority and responsibility, the Enugu State government and other state governments will be more interested in trying to generate revenue locally for education and other services than merely waiting for federal allocations from Abuja.

I know that some would argue that the Federal Government would have adequate resources for education and other services if corruption is eliminated. That may be true, but we must recognize that too much centralization and concentration of resources is itself a source of corruption. Besides, the federating units must have the autonomy to plan their development as they see fit, considering their peculiar needs and priorities. Why must lecturers in Port Harcourt or Lagos earn the same amount of money as those in Nsukka or Gombe? Is the cost of living the same everywhere in this country?

Why can't universities determine the pay of their teachers and staff? Why should it be determined in Abuja? What is the incentive for UNN or any other university to work hard at generating revenue from its alumni and other sources, if some distant agency determines its cost structure and sends it the money to pay? In better organized societies, universities such as UNN, ABU, OAU, UI and UNILAG would be generating enormous amounts of resources from their alumni because of their relative long history and production of many eminent and illustrious alumni or from their investments. Would we be having the constant disruption of the academic calendar and the associated waste of students' and parents' resources arising from the persistent disputes between the ASUU and other unions and the Federal Government? Why would private universities be the only places to have uninterrupted academic programs in a country that wants to be taken seriously?

Decentralization will help local authorities plan and implement educational and training policies and programs that best meet their local needs. Those needs are not necessarily the same in Jada in Adamawa state, Nkanu in Enugu state or Koko in Delta State.

In addition to decentralization and geographical diversification, we must also diversify our curriculum and educational programmes. The current one-size-fits-all approach will not help us. It is critical for our educational system to have a healthy mix of academic and vocational training to cater to the diverse needs of our youth and our emerging economy. I will even go further and say that key industry players should have an input into curriculum design so that there's more synergy between what our schools produce and the human resource needs of our key employers. This could be in the form of the establishment of specialized schools, with financial and other support from those key and interested private sector players.

These, in my view, are the kinds of messages that our communications media ought to be promoting in the interest of our youth and children and our country. This approach, I think, should also guide the media as they address other issues of development in Nigeria and Africa. They should guide the mass communications departments in our schools in their efforts to teach, mentor, and produce competent graduates of mass communications, ready and able to contribute to national development and their improvement as individuals. As media and communications practitioners, teachers and students, you have a responsibility to promote education, national development, evidence-based analysis and discourse, and good role models.

Tiv Dancers

You have a responsibility to promote and uphold equity in society among ethnic, religious and regional groups. This also requires discussing our differences in creative and productive ways, aimed at helping to heal and unite, rather than hurt and dismember our communities and our country. You have a responsibility to uphold and promote the rule of law, and anti-corruption and accountability. You have a responsibility to help promote ideas for building an economy for the 21st century, a post-oil economy that empowers and protects our youth; an economy that has diverse sources of revenues and employment generation; an economy that prioritizes not just oil but agriculture, solid minerals, manufacturing and services. Right now, Malaysia is seriously planning on making a transition to a post-manufacturing, knowledge-based economy just like the advanced countries of the world. Let us get serious, please.

This conference will be very helpful if it includes a deliberation on ways to ensure that our more than 10 million out-of-school Nigerian children (and millions more elsewhere in Africa) are in school. You should also be able to suggest ways in which we can reduce the poverty rate in the continent, with Nigeria's currently estimated to be up to 70% as well as our high unemployment rate, which has been helping to fuel the insecurity of life and property across the country (and indeed the continent). You may also wish to deliberate on practical steps that we need to take, to promote trade among African countries to help our people generate employment and create more wealth.

My dear friends, communication is at the centre of human interaction. It can make or mar a nation or peoples. It can create or break bonds; it can sow love or hate; it can promote equity or injustice; it can help to expose or cover up misdeeds. It can be cautious or caustic; it can lead to an embrace or repulsion. Therefore, communication is something that must be handled boldly but with caution, with the overall improvement of the human condition at its core.

To our youth I say: get an education; acquire useful skills; become aware; dream big; and aim for your dream. Do not constrain yourselves; and do not settle for half-measures. Follow your heart; the road may be rough but then only rough roads lead to somewhere desirable. Opportunities abound in this country's economy and in the economy of the 21st century, which we should be building.

Petty trading is important as a means of livelihood but it is not the only option for the young men of this South East geo-political zone. Everyone should get an education. We live in a dynamic world, a world of change and of progress. It has been called a global village because the far reaches of the world have been brought closer to each other by the revolution in communication and transportation. It is the world of the cell phone, the Internet, supercomputers, nanotechnology, 3D printing, DNA sequencing and other cutting-edge technological breakthroughs.

We must help our youth to find their path in this world or the one they will help create. We should then help them to follow that path with enthusiasm, commitment, fidelity and dedication. The media can help our young people by exposing bad deeds, promoting good deeds, highlighting good people and good deeds. That way we can help our youth to help change the world for the better.

Whether we like it or not the future belongs to our youth, especially our educated youth. Even the present is for their preparation to inherit that future.

I sincerely thank the organizers of this event, in particular the Department of Mass Communications of this storied university which is hosting it, for inviting me to be part of this conference.

Thank you for your attention and God bless.

"Change will not come if we wait for some other person or some other time. We are the ones we've been waiting for. We are the change that we seek."

Barack Obama

10 AN AGENDA FOR THE NATIONAL CONFERENCE

At Nasarawa State University Campus, 1 April, 2014

It is rather interesting that I have been asked to come here and speak on an agenda for the forthcoming National Conference, after I had publicly expressed reservations about the conference. Some of you may recall that I expressed misgivings about this conference, especially regarding its timing and whether the government has the capacity to manage the conference as well as the impending general elections. The conference ought to have been convoked a long time ago to give enough time for the outcome of its deliberations - the agreed outcomes - to have the force of law, especially as some may require the arduous process of amending our constitution. It is also a conference that may inflame passions at a time of growing tensions in the country over the 2015 general elections, governance and generalized insecurity in the land. Therefore, engaging in it now seems rather unfortunate.

The government's goal regarding the conference is also not clear to me. Let me also say that the legal framework of the conference is not clear. However, I want to assume that a new and improved Nigeria is the goal, and I believe that any opportunity for people to talk is better than to fight.

Therefore, whatever one's misgivings are, a conference has been convoked by Mr. President and it has commenced proceedings. A report or reports will be prepared and submitted, which will become part of the public record. Even if the outcome does not have the force of law, if consensus exists on that outcome, it can secure legal and legislative backing, if not now, definitely in the future.

Renewing Our Federalism

And I want to believe that this conference was motivated by the need to satisfy the yearnings of those calling for a national conference of one type or the other. At the core of those calls has been the desire to renew our federalism, to make it work. Some have called it the national question; others call it restructuring.

Obviously, our federation is not working well, and has not worked well for a long time. Indeed, it is safe to say that it is broken, and, therefore, needs fixing.

Each delegate or delegation will have expectations of the outcomes of the conference, which may be different from those of others. But if Nigeria and Nigerians are placed first (and that is a big 'if'), the outcome will be useful. But if, as some suspect, the conference is intended to sidestep the constitutional requirement for general elections in 2015 for some other arranged constitutional or transitional contraption, then the fate of similar conferences in our recent memory will befall this one as well. Nigerians, including the conference delegates, must defend our constitution and our democracy.

It is critical to achieve national consensus on key issues that will help this country and our people. Delegates may choose to focus on regional, ethnic and religious grievances; they may choose to focus on all our development and nation-building challenges. These are all important. To me, however, the agenda should be limited to a few critical issues that need to be urgently addressed in order for us to adequately confront our development challenges such as economic diversification, youth employment, security, education and infrastructure. Therefore, delegates should focus on the structure of the relations among the tiers of government (local, state and federal), that would best ensure the optimal solution to our development challenges and deepen and secure our democracy. And a great deal of the issues around this would not even require constitutional amendment.

Many different groups have representations at the conference. Ethnic nationalities have been meeting and strategizing on what to ask for. But we should not waste time asking for what nobody will give and confirming the fears of those who say this will just be a jamboree and waste of time and money. And delegates must not play into the hands of those, who plan to use the conference to precipitate crisis that would make the 2015 elections 'untenable'. I do believe that there are things we can easily agree on if only we are willing to listen to each other. There is a need to start with what we can agree on and deal with more controversial issues later.

What We Can Agree On

Nigeria is not working and part of the problem is the way we have structured our country and governance, especially since the emergence of military rule in 1966. We can agree that the Federal Government is too big, too rich, and too strong, relative to the federating states. We can agree that there is too much centralization of resources and concentration of power at the federal level.

Nigerians would not have been calling for a national conference, sovereign or not, if we were meeting our people's basic needs, including food, shelter, education, security, energy, and transportation infrastructure. They would not be calling for a conference if we were putting the country on the right path and every segment of the country feels equitably treated. And we would unlikely see people describing as a mistake, the amalgamation of the Northern and Southern parts of Nigeria, one hundred years ago.

Unitary Federalism

Thus, many of our challenges are governance issues which can be tackled by a serious government, committed to uplifting our people. Therefore, the National Conference should focus on designing a political and governmental system that empowers local authorities and gives them greater autonomy to address peculiar local issues, and enhances accountability, while contributing to the general good of the country. Such a robust federal system would reduce the tensions that are built into our current over-centralized system. While the relationships among Nigeria's ethnic and religious groups are important, the National Conference cannot expect to create a federating structure that coheres with our ethnic identities. Those identities are not only numerous but cross-cutting as well. Although our regional arrangement in the First Republic was not perfect - and did have its tensions - it certainly made for more local autonomy and better quality governance than what we have today.

Our current structure, which can best be described as 'unitary federalism' (a contradiction in terms), was created under our military regimes in the context of rising ethnic tensions and violence, an unfortunate civil war and the sudden rise in revenues from crude oil rents. As more power was concentrated in the centre, the Federal Government appropriated more resources and expanded its responsibilities. All of these were done in the name of promoting national unity. And the process was relatively easy as the unified command structure of the military ensured little opposition. Military governors/administrators in the states could not defend greater autonomy for their states against their commanders from the nation's capital: they were merely on military posting. As a corollary of Parkinson's Law, let me say that responsibility seems to expand to consume all the resources available, which, in turn, leads to the assumption of more responsibility. The more resources the Federal Government has, the more responsibilities it tends to assume, which then generates the need for even more resources.

One of the consequences of excessive centralization and the military rule that facilitated it is that the Nigerian president is probably the most powerful president in the world. This is because he could quite literally unleash all security agencies on an individual or organization, undermine the National Assembly, and turn the judiciary into an almost pro-government and conformist organ. And he can also ward off those same agencies from anyone under investigation or prosecution if the person is deemed friendly to the regime. This is not in the realm of speculation; it has been happening in this country and it has not been confined to one particular president. Therefore, fixing Nigeria, to me, will require reversing decades of over-centralization of power and over-concentration of resources at the centre. That is, it requires a degree of federal retreat. The features will include:

i. Fiscal federalism (how it will work: keep your money but I will tax)
ii. Devolution of powers to states and local government: State and local control of education, health, roads and other infrastructure (LGs to fund primary education)
iii. State and local police to augment the federal police (some say we are not ready, really?)
iv. Independence of key democratic institutions, security and anti-corruption agencies

We need to eschew emotions and knee-jerk reactions and examine these issues critically. As is to be expected, interests have been formed and entrenched so that calls for devolution and decentralization have been met with very strident opposition. In recent times, calls for these changes have come mostly from the Southern part of Nigeria, while most reactions from the Northern part of the country have tended to oppose them. It is as though the over-centralization of power and concentration of resources in the Federal Government benefit the North more than the South. Nothing can be further from the truth. In my view, and the evidence is there for all to see, the excessive dominance of the Federal Government has been detrimental to the development aspirations of all sections of this country. It is precisely why we now rely almost exclusively on oil revenues, which come mainly from a small section of the country. It is what has, by extension, killed our agriculture, local control of schools, and promoted the kind of corruption that has eroded the quality of our public and even private institutions.

I come from the North, and I can tell you that government's

reliance on oil revenues has virtually destroyed the economy of the North, and no part of Nigeria has been left unaffected. I readily acknowledge that oil money has helped us expand our infrastructure including schools, roads, and irrigation. However, if oil prices suddenly drop significantly, the country, every part of the country, will be in even more serious trouble than we are today.

Yet this is a country which, while I was growing up, had federating units that were able to send their children to school, build roads, universities, ports, factories, farm settlements, etc. I had all my formal education in Northern Nigeria and it was the Native Authority and regional government that funded it, and even paid me to go to school. Three of our first-generation universities, UNN, ABU and OAU were built by the then regional governments.

We must refrain from the habit of assuming that anyone calling for the restructuring of our federation is working for the breakup of the country. The notion that over-centralization and an excessively powerful centre is equivalent to national unity is false. If anything, it has made our unity more fragile and our government more unstable. We must renegotiate our union in order to make it stronger. Greater autonomy, power and resources for states and local authorities will unleash our people's creative energies and spur more development. It will help with improving security. It will help give the federating units and local governments greater freedom and flexibility to address local issues, priorities and peculiarities. It will promote healthy rivalries among the federating units and local authorities. It will help make us richer and stronger as a nation.

In addition to devolution of powers from the centre, the conference should also examine the wisdom of retaining the current 36-state structure. In place of the current structure of states that are too weak and hardly viable, we should revisit Dr. Alex Ekwueme's proposal during the 1994-95 Constitutional Conference for the country to adopt the six geo-political zones as the federating units. I acknowledge that I was one of those who opposed Ekwueme's proposal at the time in the mistaken belief that he wanted to break up the country. Let us consider restructuring our federation based on the current six geo-political zones as regions and the states as provinces.

Let us look at our First Republic Constitution for guidance. It is a constitution that resulted from hard bargaining among our leaders then, leaders whom no one would accuse of lacking in patriotism or developmental zeal. Let us look at our history. For example, the history of our education management and social provisioning in the First Republic and compare that with the current situation. Let us also look at other working federations around the world such as the United States, Canada, and India. What we will learn from them is that states or provinces and local municipalities have greater autonomy over their resources, development choices, and wage structures, among other things. There is no reason for the governor of Lagos State to earn the same salary as the governor of Kogi State or for a teacher in Mubi to earn the same salary as the one in Abuja or Port Harcourt, given the widely varying costs of living, productivity, and revenue generating capacities across the country.

In a nutshell, the outcome of the national conference should produce proposals that enable us to have:

- A smaller, leaner Federal Government with reduced responsibilities

Eyo Masquerade

- A tax- focused revenue base
- A true federal system which allows the component states to keep their resources but allows the Federal

- Government taxing powers
- Greater autonomy for the component states and localities to control their resources, and determine their development priorities, wage structures, and security, among other things.

Let me conclude by pointing out that even if, through the work of the National Conference, we are able to restructure and renew our federalism, Nigerians have a responsibility to elect leaders who will keep faith with the new reality and hold those leaders accountable. AS is evident, that requires genuine electoral reform, largely along the lines recommended by the Justice Mohammed Uwais Committee on electoral reform.

I thank the organizers of this event for inviting me to share my thoughts with you and I thank you for your attention.

"It is never smart even in a strong democracy to declare some debates off limits in a weakening democracy it is catastrophic."

Naomi Wolf

11 THE NEED FOR INVESTMENTS IN HEALTHCARE

Opening remarks at the 3rd Progressive Governance Lecture Series, Owerri, 1 September, 2014

I welcome all of you to Owerri, the beautiful capital of Imo State, in the Igbo heartland. This is the 3rd Progressive Governance Lecture.

Those of you who have attended the previous two lectures in this series know them to be serious gatherings, featuring erudite presentations and robust debates. I am sure that today's will be equally enriching.

The theme of today's lecture is very appropriate and timely indeed. What better time to discuss healthcare in Nigeria than now that the country is struggling to contain the highly virulent Ebola virus disease! This disease has been ravaging some of our sister countries in West Africa and has taken some precious Nigerian lives already. I am sure that I speak for all when I say that our hearts go out to those Nigerians who have become victims of this illness, just by doing their job of trying to save lives. I particularly commend the secretariat of the Progressive Governors' Forum for the foresightedness, timeliness and relevance of this topic.

The arrival of the Ebola disease has drawn attention to what we have always known: the urgent need for adequate investments in healthcare infrastructure and service delivery across the country, as well as improved communication on health and other matters.

In a way, we are lucky as a country that the Ebola challenge was brought into our country via a progressive state, one that takes governance seriously, and has, therefore, taken quite impressive steps to contain the Ebola scourge. The Federal Ministry of Health and the Federal Government took a cue from Lagos and have, so far, exceeded my expectations of them in the management of the Ebola challenge. I commend them as well.

But beyond Ebola, we have a central challenge of providing for the good health of our people. A government exists primarily to protect and provide for the welfare of its citizens; otherwise it loses its reason for existence. Incidentally, security and healthcare are two of the areas in which we are currently facing urgent and grave challenges. We are not providing adequate security for our people; and we are failing to provide good healthcare and education for our people. And the very high rate of unemployment and poverty only make matters worse.

Our doctor-to-patient ratio of 1 to 6,400 is far below the WHO standard of 1 to 600. At 54% access to improved water source and 35% access to adequate sanitation for our people, Nigeria is among the lowest in the world. Figures for infant mortality and maternal mortality of 74 and 630 respectively put us among the worst in the world. Even in Africa, we do not rank well on all these indices, which is a shame, to say the least.

Health is not a privilege. Every citizen in a modern society has a right to health care at an affordable price. Not only is the provision of healthcare the right thing for every government to do, it is also important for society to have a healthy populace which ensures a supply of healthy and productive workforce as well as consumers.

We must invest in primary health care and in preventive health care. We must provide more health enlightenment for our people. In the 21st Century, we should not have been woken up at 2am and ordered by a text message of unknown provenance to soak ourselves in salty water and to drink more than a pinch of it to fight a spreading virus. We must communicate better.

I hope that today's lecture and the discussions that will follow will enable us to come up with clear policy and governance directions for all stakeholders to buy in. We must agree on a minimum standard of care for our people, including how that will be paid for. Our approach ought to go beyond simply building hospitals and clinics but to understanding the complex array of interconnected factors that affect health and well-being and the implications of an unhealthy populace for society.

In my view, we need to identify the few illnesses that affect our people the most, what causes them and how they can be prevented. We ought to then identify priority areas that would affect the largest number of our population and tailor public policy accordingly.

What role does poverty and inhospitable environment play in our people's well-being or lack thereof? Consider these facts: the top four killers of our people are malaria, HIV/AIDS, influenza & pneumonia, and diarrhoea-related illnesses. These four account for nearly 50% of all deaths in Nigeria, and they are largely preventable. You can see then that a health care system that provides anti-malaria tablets to a patient who then goes back to the mosquito-infested slum, where she lives is not an effective one. And it is also inadequate to provide antibiotics to a patient suffering from typhoid fever who then has to go back to drinking and washing with dirty, unhealthy water because of the absence of wholesome water in his neighbourhood.

We must also, as progressives, pay attention to simple health solutions that cost little to nothing to the public purse. For instance, are we doing enough to enlighten our people to the benefits of hygiene such as simple regular washing of hands with soap, which has been shown to significantly reduce the number of hospital visits by people?

Should we continue to have a healthcare system bereft of highly qualified and experienced medical professionals while those we trained at great public expense continue to practice abroad, where they get better pay, work tools and working conditions? Can we not come up with creative solutions in our states that would lure many of these professionals back to help improve our healthcare system and our people's lives? We are a federal system. Therefore, a state or a number of states can introduce policies that make their states the place that doctors want to live and work in. I have repeatedly argued that there is no justification for workers everywhere in the country to earn the same salary. Lagos is not the same as Lokoja; Potiskum is not the same as Port Harcourt; and Yola is not the same as Yenogoa. Besides, state governments that can generate more resources internally should be able to pay their workers more and provide more facilities. Would this not likely spur more competition among states and lead to overall improvement across the country?

Is it also not high time we established real centres of excellence in healthcare in the different zones of the country such as state-of-the-art hospitals and health and disease control research centres? I believe that we have the resources; we just need the leadership, vision and determination to make these happen.

Ours are mostly governors of good example. We must continue to provide good examples for the rest of the country. Our people need them; our country needs them.

Thank you for your attention.

Borno Durbar

"Nigeria is not working as well as it should. Part of the reason is the way we have structured our country and governance, especially since the late 1960's. The Federal Government is too big, and too powerful, relative to the federating states. That situation needs to change, And calling for that change is patriotic."

Atiku Abubakar

12 RESTRUCTURING FOR NIGERIA'S NATIONAL UNITY

At the Public Presentation of the Book, "We Are All Biafrans", Abuja, 31 May, 2016

When I was invited to chair this occasion, I immediately understood that the title of the book is a metaphor for the legitimate feelings of marginalization by diverse segments of Nigerians that cut across the country. Agitations by many right-thinking Nigerians call for a restructuring and renewal of our federation to make it less centralized, less suffocating and less dictatorial in the affairs of our country's constituent units and localities.

As some of you may know, I have for a long time advocated the need to restructure our federation. Our current structure and the practices it has encouraged have been a major impediment to the economic and political development of our country. In short, it has not served Nigeria well, and at the risk of reproach, it has not served my part of the country, the North, well. The call for restructuring is even more relevant today in light of the governance and economic challenges facing us. And the rising tide of agitations, some militant and violent, require a reset in our relationships as a united nation. Some may say that we are saddled with more urgent challenges, including rebuilding our battered economy, creating jobs, fighting corruption and securing our people from terrorism and other forms of serious crimes. I believe, however, that addressing the flaws in our federation will help us address some of those very economic and security challenges facing this country.

Nigeria must remain a united country. Our potentials are enormous. But I also believe that a united country, which I think most Nigerians desire, should never be taken for granted or taken as evidence that Nigerians are content with the current structure of the federation. Making that mistake might set us on the path of losing the country we love or, as Chido Onumah puts it, result in our "country sleepwalking to disaster."

Let me quickly acknowledge that no federal system is set for all time. There are always tensions arising from matters relating to the sharing of power, resources and responsibilities. But established democracies have developed peaceful mechanisms for resolving such conflicts among the tiers of government. They recognize that negotiations and compromises are eternal.

How We Got Here: Oil Economy, Centralization and Biafranization

The vast majority of Nigeria's young population will be forgiven for thinking that our lives have always revolved around oil and that the Federal Government has always been this domineering and controlling. They may not be aware that the federal system which we inherited at independence allowed the regions to retain their autonomy to raise and retain revenues, promote development, and conduct their affairs as they saw fit, while engaging in healthy competition with others.

And they may not know that it was the emergence of military rule and the intervening civil war that led to the splintering and weakening of the federating units, centralization of resources and concentration of power at the federal level. The enormous revenues from oil rents encouraged the central government to play an increasingly domineering role in the economy and society. It assumed more responsibilities for infrastructure provisioning, education, social services and business investment.

We now know that the more resources the Federal Government has, the more responsibilities it tends to assume. This then generates the need for even more resources. As chairman of the National Council on Privatization from 1999 to 2007, in my capacity as the vice president, I was shocked when I saw first-hand the manner of businesses our Federal Government was involved in. These included not just such capital-intensive industries as steel and petrochemicals but brick-making factories and bakeries as well. These enterprises hardly made any profit. Rather, they were being subsidized by the budget.

As the government's role continued to expand, the private sector was crowded out and private initiative, innovation and creativity suffered; excessive dependence on oil revenues led to the collapse of our agriculture-based economy. It also exposed the Nigerian economy to volatile market swings, booms and bursts. And it brought with it enormous social consequences such as wealth without labour, briefcase contractors and generations of youth accustomed to aspiring to be employed by others rather than thinking of creating jobs for themselves and others. It also led to the neglect of internally generated revenue, especially taxation. Most of our state governments can no longer pay their workers' wages until they collect monthly allocations from Abuja. Only Lagos State is currently able to generate up to 50% of its revenues internally, thereby reducing its dependence on allocation from Abuja. (And it is not because of the existence of many businesses in Lagos as some people like to point out. Businesses do not on their own send money to government).

As we became more dependent on oil revenues we became lazier, more complacent, and our leaders became ever more unaccountable. Among the most destructive impact of our dependence on oil is, perhaps, the corruption that it has fostered in the oil industry and society at large. Some of you are familiar with published reports that highlight discrepancies and opacity in data relating to the allocation of oil blocs as well as NNPC's abuse of its duty as steward of our federation revenues. The result of all of this is that we have not made the needed investments in human capital development and the productive sectors of the economy. According to the Human Development Index, 70% of our population lives below the poverty line compared to 21.4% for Brazil, 40.5% for Angola and 0% for Norway, to mention a few comparable oil producing countries.

More critical is the distortion of our federal structure by our dependence on oil. We now have the ridiculous situation, where the Federal Government creates local governments, enshrines them in the constitution and allocates resources directly to them, with people even calling for more autonomy from state governments.

Today virtually every section of our country feels marginalized – meaning, they believe that other segments of society are prospering in ways they are not. We often interpret marginalization along regional, ethnic or religious lines, but experience has shown that this perception can exist even within homogenous communities due to uneven access to opportunity. For example, we have communities feeling marginalized within their states or regions.

Having established the 'federal character' of marginalization in Nigeria, it is imperative that our response to the issues raised by our various 'Biafrans' across the country is holistic.

I have long advocated for greater autonomy, powers and resources for our federating states. Some have retorted that state governors will abuse those powers and resources. Well the same logic applies to the federal level, which, as recent revelations show, is not without blemish. In fact, the current situation encourages governors to abuse their power, do little to raise revenue and point fingers at the federal government, thereby making it more difficult for their people to hold them to account.

What do we need?

- First, a smaller, leaner Federal Government with reduced responsibilities. This means devolution of powers and resources to states and local governments. State and local governments should control education, health, agriculture, roads and other infrastructure. A true federal system will allow the federating states to keep their resources while the federal government retains the power of taxation and regulatory authority over standards. The result will be a political and governmental system that empowers local authorities and gives them greater autonomy to address peculiar local issues, while enhancing accountability and contributing to the general good of the country. Such a robust federal system would reduce the tensions that are built into our current over-centralized system.

- Second, autonomy for the component states and localities to determine their development priorities and wage structures. For instance, there is no reason for the governor of Akwa Ibom State to earn the same salary as the governor of Benue State or for a teacher in Orlu to earn the same salary as the one in Abuja or Port Harcourt. The costs of living and revenue generating capacities vary widely across the country.

- Third, a tax-centred revenue base. Modern democracies derive their revenues from taxation whether or not they have fossil fuels and other natural resources - personal income tax, property tax, sales tax, corporate tax, licences, and duties. Taxation is a sustainable revenue base and one that compels governments to promote increased economic activities, and respond to the demands of their tax-paying citizens.

- Fourth, enhanced, diversified economic activities and productivity in order to enlarge the tax base. The US, UK, Canada, Malaysia, and UAE are all oil producers. But because they have diversified economies, oil does not dominate their government revenues and does not have the same distortionary effect it has on our own. Let's compare Malaysia with Nigeria. Both countries were at a comparable level of development at independence but now Malaysia's GDP per capita is $11,000 while Nigeria's is $3,000. Malaysia has foreign reserves of $100 billion and a sovereign wealth fund of $41 billion. In Malaysia, manufacturing accounts for 40% of GDP and the country is rated the 14th most competitive economy in the world.

- In Nigeria, however, manufacturing accounts for a mere 10% of GDP, and only 12% of the labour force. And

Nigeria ranks 127th out of 144 in global competitiveness. Think about this for a moment: If the bulk of the revenues of our federal and state governments are dependent on the level of economic activities in the country, would we be shutting down the entire country or a state on election days, on census days and during environmental clean-up? I wish some of our researchers would calculate the resulting loss of productivity and incomes to individuals, families and the economy, and, therefore, potentially government revenues.

- Fifth, an end to the indigene-settler dichotomy. A modern united Nigerian society can only be built on the basis of common citizenship for all based on residency in a state or locality rather than the local government or ethnic group one is born into. Nigerians should be free to live, study and work anywhere in the country as long as they are law-abiding. We cannot claim to be promoting national unity while also promoting policies that tend to confine people to their places of birth.

- Sixth, state police to augment the federal police (for the states that so desire). This will help us to improve security, including fighting terrorism. Posting a police officer from Ganye to Eket may help promote culture sharing and integration, but it does little to prevent or fight crime. Crime is better fought by those who know the terrain and speak the local language.

Ladies and gentlemen, Nigeria is not working as well as it should and part of the reason is the way we have structured our country and governance, especially since the late 1960's. The Federal Government is too big, and too powerful, relative to the federating states. That situation needs to change, and calling for that change is patriotic.

We must refrain from the habit of assuming that anyone calling for the restructuring of our federation is working for the breakup of the country. An excessively powerful centre does not equate with national unity. If anything, it has made our unity more fragile, our government more unstable and our country more unsafe. We must renegotiate our union in order to make it stronger. Greater autonomy, power and resources for states and local authorities will give the federating units greater freedom and flexibility to address local issues, priorities and peculiarities. It will help to unleash our people's creative energies and spur more development. It will reduce the premium placed on capturing power at the centre. It will help with improving security. It will promote healthy rivalries among the federating units and local authorities. It will help make us richer and stronger as a nation.

I commend the author, Chido Onumah, for his efforts at putting his thought-provoking writings together in this book. I hope that the essays contained therein will help to stir and deepen the debates on our federal structure, governance and intergovernmental relations. Hopefully those debates will help us effect the needed changes to make our country realize its full potentials in peace and greater harmony. This is an important way to prevent the birth and growth of Biafrans across our dear country.
Thank you.

Agbaka Cultural Group

"We must work with determination to create a society
Not where men are superior and other men are inferior and vice versa,
But a society in which all men will live together as brothers
And Respect the dignity and worth of human personality."

Martin Luther King

13 ENTREPRENEURSHIP AND THE POST-OIL NIGERIAN ECONOMY

At the National Conference on Entrepreneurship, Abuja, 26 July 2016

I am pleased to have the opportunity to address this Orji Uzor Kalu Foundation Conference focused on entrepreneurship. You have chosen an interesting and quite appropriate theme. As Nigerians, we have since the early 1980's, been grappling with the issue of what would drive the Nigerian economy in the post-oil era.

Some have stressed a return to agriculture, which accounted for the bulk of government revenues before oil and which still employs the majority of our people and accounts for the bulk of our GDP. Others have stressed solid minerals, and the manufacturing or services sectors. In short, everyone recognizes the need for us to diversify our economy away from dependence on oil revenues.

But, as the theme of this conference suggests, ultimately, the key is entrepreneurship, whatever sector or sectors we emphasize: our seeming addiction to revenues from oil rents has somewhat dulled our entrepreneurial spirit.

Entrepreneurship is the process of designing, starting and running a business. It is having the desire and capacity to develop, organize and manage a business enterprise, with the associated risks, in order to make a profit. The entrepreneur is the person or team that identifies a business opportunity and takes risks in making investments in an economic activity, with the hope of realizing profits. Such investments include capital and human resources.

Entrepreneurship is what creates private wealth, jobs, innovation, and builds an economy. The roles of such great entrepreneurs as J.P. Morgan, C. Vanderbilt, John D. Rockefeller, A. Carnegie and Henry Ford in building the American economy are well documented. Governments tax the income and wealth of entrepreneurs and workers to provide such public goods and services as security, defence, infrastructure, health care, education, regulation, funding of primary research, and international affairs (diplomacy). These, in turn, help to promote more economic activities, thereby producing more wealth for people and the society.

Entrepreneurship is in the blood of Nigerians and, I suspect, all of humanity. We have a long history of production and trade among our various communities, including long distance trade across the length and breadth of the present-day Nigeria and beyond. And when colonialism brought the modern capitalist economy, we embraced it. The exploits of the likes of Philip Odumegwu Ojukwu, Alhassan Dantata, Adeola Odutola and others are well known. I need not reel out the names of the numerous young and older Nigerians today, who are astute entrepreneurs, helping to build the Nigerian (indeed African) economy and putting Nigeria on the global business map.

But the emergence of oil as the dominant revenue source for government led to the creation of wealth that we did not have to work for. Thus, rather than build on the legacies of the earlier entrepreneurs, we became contractors for government. Rather than encourage innovation and entrepreneurship in our people, our governments became content with sharing money from oil. As we stopped working, government itself stopped collecting taxes, the real source of sustainable government revenues around the world. Only those whose taxes are deducted at source continued to pay taxes.

These notwithstanding, oil rents ensured that government revenues skyrocketed. This gave the government the impetus to centralize more power and concentrate more resources at the centre, at the expense of the constituent states. The states became dependent on the centre. Therefore, all tiers of government became dependent on and addicted to oil money. The government pursued statist economic policies and practices which saw it engage directly in the economy as an investor. The Federal Government directly invested not only in capital intensive ventures such as petrochemicals and automotive manufacturing but also in such simple tasks as brick-making and bread baking.

The central government became overbearing, even intervening in local governance by arrogating to itself the power to create local governments all over the country and even enshrined them in the constitution. Changes by the federating states are, therefore, virtually impossible. As a result, the private sector was crowded out; entrepreneurship suffered. There was little innovation and investment in productive activities.

Mr. Chairman, ladies and gentlemen, the wild up-and-down swings in the price of oil and the accompanying economic crises, including the current one, continue to brutally remind us to change course. We can no longer afford to forget our experience and revert to our bad habits after the depths of each crisis.

What we need, therefore, is a shift towards entrepreneurship as the driving force for our economic development and wealth and job creation. Such a course will involve designing a post-oil economic strategy for Nigeria.

Oil will likely remain important for a while longer but it is safe to assume that the oil economy has reached its peak. This is because of the efforts towards alternative energy sources around the world, as well as improvements in the technology of oil production which has led to increased oil production and depressed prices.

We must, therefore, chart a post-oil course for our country. We need to awaken the entrepreneurial tiger in our people. It will require a lot of work, a lot of structural changes in our economy and politics, a lot of sacrifices and compromises by interested groups, as well as supportive international developments. My fear though is that while we dither, the rest of the oil consuming world would leave us behind as they transition to a future without much use for fossil fuels. Just last month, the US, Canada and Mexico - all major oil producers - pledged to derive 50% of their energy from clean sources by 2025.

Putting Oil in its Proper Context

On the surface, there is nothing wrong with oil revenues. The problem is the potential of oil rents to distort an economy, politics, and governance. In Nigeria for instance, three states account for 80% of the oil production. Oil accounts for 90% of exports and 95% of government revenues. The oil industry contributes little in direct employment relative to its contribution to government revenues. Politically, oil money is easy money as governments do not need to go to the people for revenues in the form of taxation. Thus, internally generated revenue sources, especially taxation, are neglected and contribute very little to government revenues. And a source of the crisis in the Nigerian society and politics is the question of revenue allocation among the federating states. The tensions generated by this imbalance would be less if the sources of government revenues are diverse both in content and in geography. And we all know of the pervasive corruption which oil money has facilitated in the country, as various reports and studies make clear.

Oil constitutes only a small portion of our GDP and, therefore, need not be the dominant source of government revenues. Indeed exports, of which oil is the dominant part, do not even contribute the bulk of our GDP and, therefore, need not be the dominant source of government revenues. It is how we have collected, allocated and distributed those revenues that have shaped our economy and society since the late 1960s. We must change those.

Promoting Entrepreneurship and Sustainable Development
In my view, in order for us to run our country in a sustainable way, we must do the following:

1. Promote entrepreneurship the way other modern democracies do, whether or not they have fossil fuels and other natural resources. In other words, we must promote activities that ensure we derive government revenues from sustainable sources, primarily taxation — personal income tax, property tax, sales tax, corporate tax, licenses, and duties. A large and diverse tax base requires increased economic activities and a determination, and the mechanisms to collect the taxes. Politically, funding governance through taxation ensures government can only spend what citizens can bear. And it has the added advantage of helping foster accountability. Entrepreneurs and workers are more likely to demand accountability if the cost of governance comes directly from their pockets rather than from some impersonal or detached revenue sources such as oil rent.

   This conference may want to deliberate on the importance of setting targets regarding sources of government revenue away from oil rents as well as the modalities for meeting them. In my view, that may encourage government to do more to promote entrepreneurship and other economic activities. Government has the greatest capacity to promote entrepreneurship and the more entrepreneurial activities that go on, the more income, businesses and workers will likely earn and the more taxes that government would be able to collect. As you know, over the long-term, businesses will make profits, and if they do, government revenues, through taxation, are likely to grow as long as the government is willing to levy and collect the taxes.

2. Diversification of the economy and promotion of entrepreneurship will involve massive investments in the improvement of infrastructure which will spur private

investments, the key creator of jobs. Can anyone imagine what would have happened if we had multi-lane highways running along the Atlantic Coast from Port Harcourt to Lagos, and along the coasts of River Niger and River Benue, throughout the areas that they traverse this vast country. How many hotels and restaurants and other businesses would domestic and foreign investors have built along those highways? How many homes would have been built as a result? How many farms would have been established? What if we have rail lines linking all the states of this country? Would it not have been easier to transport people and goods across the country? Does anybody know the amount of tourism those investments would spur?

You may want to deliberate on more effective ways in which the private sector can be encouraged to participate in the provision of infrastructure. Our private sector has grown significantly over the years, that it is in a position to complement government efforts. In the 1960s and even 1970s, virtually no indigenous private company could build a major highway, or a university, or cement factory or powder plant, but there are many that can do so now.

However, in order to thrive, the private sector needs an entrepreneurial environment, including supportive and stable macro-economic and regulatory frameworks, promotion of risk-taking and the encouragement of and reward for basic research. You may also want to deliberate on what the likes of the US, U.K., Canada, Malaysia, and UAE - all big oil producers - did and do differently to ensure that oil does not dominate their economies and politics as it does here.

3. Promoting entrepreneurship will involve huge investments in human capital development, which is every modern nation's most important resource. We must reform, expand and better fund education, including business education, improve healthcare delivery, and improve security. Your conference may also want to discuss ways in which our nation can do these more effectively.

4. The diversification of the economy away from oil will be helped by a significant reduction in the level of centralization and concentration of power and resources in the Federal Government. More power, resources, and responsibilities should be ceded to the states and local governments and they should be allowed to develop at their own pace and in accordance with local conditions. The idea of governors simply coming to Abuja to share money every month, to even be able to pay salaries is very destructive of our economy and politics. What's the incentive to promote economic activities and look for other sources of revenue when there is 'free' money to be shared? A country that shuts down an entire economy because it wants to conduct census or elections or environmental clean-up is obviously not one that promotes and values productivity.

Ladies and gentlemen, as you deliberate, I urge you to look forward. Do not get stuck in tried and failed ideas and practices of the 1970s and 1980s, ideas that have not really worked anywhere else in a sustained way. Help to find ways to truly promote entrepreneurship so our people can unleash their creative and productive energies. That way we can build this country into a truly productive and advanced one, able to cater to our people's welfare and security as well as enhance their freedoms, while protecting the ecosystem for future generations.

Thank you for your attention.

Ohafia Dancers

"Education is a human right with immense power to transform.
On its foundation rest the cornerstones of freedom,
democracy and sustainable human development."

Kofi Annan

14 RESTRUCTURING NIGERIA FOR GREATER NATIONAL INTEGRATION AND DEMOCRATIC STABILITY

At the late Gen. Usman Katsina Memorial Conference, Kaduna, 30 July 2016

The theme of this conference, The Challenges of National Integration and Survival of Democracy in Nigeria makes two very important acknowledgements:

1. National integration and the survival of Nigeria's democracy are related and are important;

2. They both face challenges in Nigeria today.

3. I believe that most Nigerians would agree with those propositions although we are likely to have differences regarding how to achieve national integration and ensure the survival of our democracy.

I have spoken, I think clearly and forcefully, on both issues on several occasions in the last twelve years or so. Permit me to focus on national integration in this presentation.

National integration, to me, simply means the process by which different components of a country, with economic, political and cultural links, develop a sense of nationhood, of unity, of oneness, of interdependence, irrespective of their different histories, experiences, ideologies, and cultural values and practices. Such a sense of nationhood and oneness encourages a commitment by the people to the survival of the nation and its values and principles, cultures and territorial integrity. One of those values may be democracy - that system of government, which allows citizens the freedom to choose their leaders in periodic elections, speak their minds, associate with their fellows, and puts limits on the powers of leaders.

As a country, we have mightily struggled to live up to this ideal. We have obviously not done enough to realize national integration, and the survival of our democracy is still a work in progress. The cost to us has been enormous. We even fought a civil war to forcibly keep the country together. Since the various amalgamations that created the entity that we now call Nigeria, different segments of Nigeria's population have, at different times and sometimes at the same time, expressed feelings of marginalization, of being short-changed, dominated, oppressed, threatened, or even targeted for elimination. Apart from regional, ethnic and religious groupings, other segments of the population such as labour and professional groups have expressed similar frustrations arising from a sense of exclusion and helplessness. This often stems from feelings that their voices are not being heard or that they are unable to hold those in power to account. There is also a sense of disengagement of large portions of the population, especially due to high rate of youth unemployment and lack of obvious economic opportunities.

We have over the years responded to these agitations in a

variety of ways and with a variety of measures. These include the creation of states from the earlier three (and later four) regions to the current 36 states; a civil war, and other military operations in different parts of the country at different times; federal character principle; changes to revenue allocation formula; National Youth Service Corps; federal take-over or establishment and management of schools, universities, hospitals, and huge federal presence in the economy as an investor. Others include the excessive centralization and concentration of power at the federal level and the weakening of the federating states and amnesty for ''repentant ex-militants" of the Niger Delta.

Unfortunately, these measures have not worked adequately to enhance national integration and the sustenance of our democracy. If anything, our unity has been fragile, our democracy unstable, and our people more aggrieved by their state in the federation. We have always responded with a suspicion of the "other", in trying to deal with these challenges to our integration and democratic survival. And, quite naturally, our responses/solutions have also been, at least partly, shaped by sectional interests and sentiments. The problem though is that sometimes what is in the short-term interest of a group may not be so in the long-run. And more importantly, nation-building requires sacrifices of some sectional interests for the overall interest of the nation and all the segments. Unless we do not think that the nation's unity is worth sacrificing for or that the sacrifices have to be made only by others and not by us!

Sometimes we implement contradictory policies that weaken national integration. An example is the requirement of state and local government of origin rather than residency for access to government services and jobs. That alone restricts people's mobility and infuses in them a sense of rejection by the very country that wants them to feel welcome and proud.

Personally, I believe in one strong and united Nigeria. I believe that we are stronger united, and that together our potentials are enormous. And I believe that Nigeria's unity is worth sacrificing for.

It is not a secret that many Nigerians from outside the North hold the view that the main beneficiary of the status quo has been the North, an undifferentiated North. Sometimes they say it is the Northern elite or the "Kaduna Mafia". This sentiment, I think, stems largely from the following reasons:

i. People of Northern extraction, being the heads of government at the national level for much of our post-independence period until 1999, during which period much of the current structure was put in place,

ii. The leading role that the North played in the war to keep the country united between 1967 and 1970,

iii. The country's reliance on oil revenues which comes mainly from the Niger Delta, far away from the North, as well as;

iv. What some see as a knee-jerk resistance from Northern elements to calls for the restructuring of the federation.

Having led the federal side in the war to keep the country together, it is understandable that Northern leaders would have less tolerance for what they perceive as another attempt to break up the country.

My focus here, however, is to show that the North and Nigeria have not been served well by the status quo and there is need for change. Who among us who went to primary and secondary school (and even university) in the 1960's had much to do with the Federal Government? Did the Northern Regional Government wait to collect monthly revenue allocations from Lagos before paying salaries to its civil servants and teachers or fixing its bridges and roads? In May, this year, the governor of Niger State publicly stated that his state could no longer pay salaries because of dwindling federal allocations. And he is not alone. A recent report by Economic Intelligence published in a number of Nigerian newspapers showed that 9 out of the 10 States with the lowest internally generated revenue are in the North. And they are among the 15 states that the report said may go bankrupt, if federal allocations to states continue to decline because their IGR is less than 10% of their federal allocations. There is something wrong with the structure of this country and we must see it for what it is. Even in the unlikely event that federal allocations are shared equally among all the states, we would still be in trouble if we cannot generate revenues internally.

How can we excuse the reality that the section of the country that produces most of the country's food (that is, the North) cannot raise revenues to cater to its internal needs? Who do we blame for having a large number of our school-age children being out of school? Why should our people continue to roam the forests with herds of cattle and sheep in the 21st century, when we have had the opportunity to take advantage of advances in the technology and science of animal rearing to settle our herds in particular spots and produce even fatter animals to meet the country's rising demand for meat and milk? This is what the rest of the organized world has done. Therefore, we need to promote diverse economic activities, tax the proceeds of those activities and use the proceeds to provide public goods and services for our people. Citizens and businesses do not generally volunteer money to governments.

It is the rising dominance of oil revenues that led us to abandon cash crop production and neglect agriculture. Before oil, agriculture was our main industry and we taxed it (and the products of other economic activities) to develop the North - to provide education, healthcare and infrastructure. But because of oil we now plead helplessness. The North has the largest known deposits of solid minerals in Nigeria, including some of the rarest and most expensive. So why should we be afraid of the concept of resource control, that is the control of rents by the areas of derivation?

My brothers and sisters, most government revenues all over the world are based on taxation. Infrastructure for economic development is built with taxation. Rents on natural resource extraction, including oil rents, are not sustainable sources of revenues for government. And whenever and wherever they are dominant for a nation, they tend to distort the economy, discourage productivity and encourage rent-seeking activities and dependency.

What should be done?

For a start, we need:

1. An honest reappraisal of the motives and principles behind existing solutions to our national integration challenges and their efficacy under current circumstances. Such an appraisal should not be shaped by which political party we belong to or any expected political benefits to individuals. It can be done with the help of a body of independent experts from this part of the country or even from outside the country.

2. An honest and clear-headed look at better working federal systems in the world. Those systems will reveal, among other things, a greater devolution and autonomy for the federating units, less interference of the centre on local matters, such as local government administration, including local policing; central governments that depend on taxation of resource extraction and other economic activities rather than rents for their operations.

I've been speaking about achieving greater national integration through devolution and decentralization for some time now because I know that too much concentration of power at the centre hurts the country and the North in at least three critical ways: (1) Destroying our economy and values as it does elsewhere; (2) Putting too much premium on the struggle for power at the centre; and (3) Creating the false perception that the North benefits from the status quo, thus presenting the North as being responsible for the country's development challenges.

There is no doubt that oil revenues have helped Nigeria (and the North) to expand infrastructure, education, and health facilities. Those benefits must be weighed against the long-term costs, including distortions, the creation of dependency and unstable politics. And the level of poverty, illiteracy, unemployment and sense of hopelessness among our people, especially the youth, gives the lie to the perception that the North is better off with the current socio-political structure in the country. Today, the price of oil is low and the country's economic survival is being threatened by groups disrupting the flow of that oil. When we look at our future in these circumstances, what exactly do we see?

The North has ample supply of people, young people. All we need to do is educate them and provide them with the skills to be competitive in the country and the world. They and the North will succeed, and if they do, Nigeria will succeed. The world of today is not one of dominance by mere numbers. The quality of those numbers is more important. The world is also not dominated by the regions with the largest deposits of natural resources. For example, Japan, which has no significant mineral deposits and little land for agriculture is the third largest economy in the world. Also, Singapore moved from being a Third World to a First World economy, despite having little in terms of natural resources.

I believe that we have reached the peak of the oil economy. Even for those who think nothing of diversifying to alternative revenue sources, the 'jamboree' is clearly over. Oil prices may still go up in real terms in the future, but the long-term trend will be downwards, and here are the reasons:

1. New technologies of oil and gas extraction, especially hydraulic fracturing (also known as fracking) have helped in pumping out more oil than the world needs. In fact, those technologies have helped to push the US

towards becoming the world's top oil producer. Is it any wonder that US import of Nigerian oil has declined to almost zero?

2. Growing investments in alternative energy sources as well as the declining costs per unit of these alternatives have not only added significantly to the world's energy mix but also appear to have set the world on an irreversible move towards reliance on non-fossil fuel and renewable energy.

Let me give you just a few examples. In 2004, the world generated only 48 gigawatts of electricity from wind power but by 2014, wind power accounted for 318 gigawatts. In 2004, only 2.6 gigawatts of power were generated worldwide from solar photovoltaic (PV), but by 2014, 139 gigawatts were being generated, and this excludes an additional 326 gigawatts thermal solar water heating capacity. Also, total annual biofuel production rose from 30.9 billion litres in 2004 to 113.5 litres by 2014. The same phenomenal increase is noticed in annual investments in renewable energy, from a mere $39.5 billion in 2004 to $214.4 billion by 2014. In 2004, only 48 countries had policy targets regarding renewable energy but by 2014, the number had reached 144. As we speak here today, cars using non-oil based energy either in full or in part are being produced for the mass market. And just last month the US, Canada and Mexico pledged to derive 50% of their energy from clean sources by 2025.

The impetus for these dramatic changes came from the various energy crises which the world has experienced since the early 1970s; the creation of critical markets for renewable energy by such pioneer countries as Germany, Denmark, Spain and the US; and the growing efforts to mitigate climate change. Of course, the declining costs of renewables arising from the increased investments and capacity have been helpful. All of these will continue to put pressure on oil prices even when the world economy fully recovers.

You can therefore see that the fight in this country over "resource control", while it may still have significance today, is really a fight that belongs to the past. Even a discovery of large quantities of oil and gas in the North today, can only bring temporary relief - it cannot reverse the fundamental shifts in the world's energy trajectory. In any case, how are we to improve this region and hold it (and the country) together in the time lag between such a discovery and actual production and revenue in-flow? I humbly submit that we need to move on like the rest of the world.

I am not trying to be a messenger of doom but to alert us to the serious challenges ahead, if we do not take immediate corrective actions both in our economics and our politics. For this region particularly, the following measures will be helpful for our economic, social and political recovery and development. Interestingly, they are also what Nigeria needs.

1. Devolution of more powers and responsibilities to the federating units with the accompanying resources currently expended on them by the Federal Government. And here I am not saying the units must be the existing states. We may have to revisit the issue of the current geo-political zones becoming federating units. This will also help put an end to the endless quest for the creation of more states, with little thought as to how those states will be financed. In any case, each federating unit can

decide to have as many local authorities as it deems fit. Education, agriculture, healthcare, roads and bridges should be the responsibility of the federating units (zones or states) while the Federal Government sets standards and enforces them.

Resources such as mining rent should belong to the federating units, where they are derived from, while the Federal Government retains the power of taxation over the corporations that are involved in their exploitation and of course, the federal portion of personal income tax. Federating units should have the right to set the wages of their employees in line with their needs and ability to pay. As our history has shown, a strong centre does not translate to a strong and united country.

2. We should begin to think strategically about how to develop this region as a collective. At the minimum, states in each geo-political zone (with or without the zones as federating units) should begin to work together to share responsibilities such as infrastructure provisioning and the running of social services such as schools and hospitals. This will help save cost and help us integrate the zones and the region more socially and economically. There is no reason why some states cannot merge their universities, polytechnics or even hospitals and run them with one administrative unit.

3. The ACF and other socio-cultural organizations based in this region should broaden their scope to include research and advocacy, to encourage the states in the North and/or in each geopolitical zone to engage in meaningful collaboration in governance. And they should produce a research-based position on the restructuring of the federation, possibly along the lines of geopolitical zones as federating units to assist political leaders and representatives of the region in understanding the issues involved and in their negotiations among themselves and with the rest of the country.

Those who argue that restructuring of the polity won't be necessary once we diversify the economy are mistaken. As long as the Federal Government remains overly dominant relative to the federating states, it will continue to matter which section of the country 'captures' federal power with its attendant instability. And as long as the Federal Government keeps the bulk of oil revenues for itself, its desire and will to provide the leadership needed to diversify the economy will continue to be limited.

I suggest we resolve today to support calls for the restructuring of the Nigerian federation to strengthen its unity and stabilize its democracy. I believe that restructuring will eventually happen whether we like or support it or not. The question is whether it will happen around a conference table, in a direction influenced by us and whether we will be an equal partner in the process. Or will it happen in a more unpredictable arena and in a manner over which we have little influence? It should be at a table and we need to be at that table. A nation is an organism; it grows, it evolves, it changes, it adapts. And like other organisms, if it does not adapt, it dies.

Mr. Chairman, ladies and gentlemen, national integration is achievable in Nigeria. But we must do the little things that will help in that regard. Apart from resolving issues around access to economic resources and power by the federating units, there are vital intangibles such as values, ideology, and a sense of investment in the nation that help in fostering a sense of national integration. It is one thing to say that Nigeria must remain a united nation. It is quite another thing to forge that sense of nationhood, without which you can never have national integration. And to forge that nationhood requires, at the very least, three critical things:

1. A sense of something beneficial that the nation does for a people that they feel they cannot get elsewhere to the same vital degree.

2. People's perception of fairness and equity in the way and manner they are treated

3. Arising from these, a sense of pride in the nation and its leadership by most segments of the population.

All three are linked to government performance, integrity of the leadership and honesty of purpose, which will be evident to the citizenry. From these, ideologies that project the nation as special can arise, and help to cement the people's commitment to it. These, to me are more effective than forcing or bribing people to stay together.

This is a gathering of major stakeholders in the Nigeria project and people here need to join that debate on restructuring. But let our positions be guided by reason, by facts, by history and by a deep reflection on what is in the best interest of our people, and the people of Nigeria, our country. Let our positions not be guided by a knee-jerk reaction that rejects every position on that matter, except the one we have held for forty or more years.

And while we are at it, let us educate our young people. Let us make sure that every child born in this part of the country goes to and stays in school until the age of 18, by which time most would have completed secondary education. Let us also support those who want to proceed to tertiary education as well as technical and vocational training. Let us prepare our youth for the challenges ahead, so they can thrive in the world of rapid technological advances, a world that is unlikely to have a viable place for the uneducated. Let's once and for all wipe out the false impression held by others that we deliberately keep our people illiterate and backward, especially because the elite among us ensure that our own children go to school.

Mr. Chairman, ladies and gentlemen, it is fitting that we are gathered here in memory of one of the illustrious sons of the North and Nigeria, the late General Hassan Usman Katsina, a man who played a critical role in our national affairs, including efforts to keep this country united. Once more, that unity is under severe stress, and statesmen must rise to the occasion and proffer solutions that are sustainable and can endure. We cannot tell a person who says he feels pain, that he does not feel pain. Rather we find out what the person says is the nature of the pain and then try to find effective remedies. Interestingly, we too feel pain and need urgent remedies.

I am grateful to the organizing committee for this conference and for inviting me to deliver this paper.

I thank you all for your attention.

"Only by restructuring can we guarantee Unity, Equity and Security for our nation."

Atiku Abubakar

Ijan Masquerade

"We have to acknowledge that federalisms are works in progress.
There is no ideal federal system or so-called true federalism.
Each nation must work out the best federal system suited for it."

Atiku Abubakar

15 THE VALUE OF EDUCATION: A PERSONAL STORY

At the Ford Foundation Special Reunion (80th Anniversary), Lagos, 1 September 2016

I would like to thank the Ford Foundation for inviting me to share my life experiences and the importance of scholarships in Nigeria. I believe the basic element of a democratic society is the empowerment of people. But that cannot be achieved without providing quality education to all our citizens.

I must confess that it is difficult to summarize a life that is still unfolding. Mine is. After all, I will only turn 70 this November. Who knows? 70 may be the new 40.

My life's story began in Jada, Adamawa State but it might as well have begun in Washington DC, where the decision was made by the US government to establish the Peace Corps 55 years ago. The Peace Corps sent many young American men and women to far-flung parts of the world to assist local communities to meet a variety of challenges, including education.

Though he later relented, my father was put in prison by local authorities for refusing to send me to school. Like many parents of his generation, he needed my help in the farm.

My encounter with Peace Corps teachers in the 1960's had a profound impact on my life. It helped to instil in me the virtues of hard work, critical thinking, and commitment to excellence. The teachers encouraged us to develop a "can-do" spirit and never to despair, in order to bring out the best in us to enable us to succeed in life. In my young eyes, those Peace Corps represented excellence. They instilled in me a burning desire to look to a wider horizon, to have a global outlook. So, my encounter with the Peace Corps changed my life. And education is responsible for the modest success I have achieved thus far.

Because of the education I received, paid for by the Northern Regional Government and local authorities, I could rise from a small village in Adamawa to the topmost levels of the Nigeria Customs Service. My exposure to education encouraged me to embrace savings and investment, from very early in my career. Upon retirement, I went into business. And when my mentor, the late General Shehu Musa Yar'Adua, invited some of us to join politics to help restore democracy to our country, I agreed, guided by that same "can-do" spirit. Since then, both in and out of public office, my commitment to democracy has not wavered.

The influence of Peace Corps on me would come into play when, with the help of friends in Nigeria and the US, I decided to establish an educational village in my home town of Yola, Adamawa State. This educational complex incorporates the levels of kindergarten to university, the American University of Nigeria, Yola. My choice of American-style education led to fruitful relationships with two universities in the US - the American

University, Washington, DC and later, Tulane University, as the AUN strives to maintain excellence. AUN has been, by far, my largest philanthropic educational undertaking. A twelve-year-old, thoroughly modern campus, and the only one with 24/7 Internet connection in Nigeria, we have the finest e-library in Africa. This university is not merely 'American' in name: we stress small interactive classes, general education, student internships, critical thinking, problem solving, and student research. In the midst of the Boko Haram crisis in our region, our students, through a community service program also unique in Nigeria, have been at the forefront of humanitarian relief and development work. Many of our students, of course, receive scholarships.
And I have continued with my long-established practice of providing scholarships to needy students across Africa.

So, ladies and gentlemen, I want to stress the following:

i. If the government did not force my father, I would not have been allowed to go to school.

ii. I could not have acquired an education if my parents were required to pay for it.

iii. Whatever modest achievements and contributions I have made, I owe to education.

iv. Perhaps we can draw some lessons from my experience.

1. If, as a society, we deem high quality education important, it must be adequately funded. Our decision about who pays has consequences.

Igbabonelimhin, Esan Cultual Dance

2. Greater local control is critical, if we are to achieve universal basic education; an education that is relevant to local communities.

3. Education should be free, accessible and compulsory at the primary and secondary levels, to give every child an opportunity to acquire education irrespective of family circumstances.

4. If a society opts for fee payments by students and parents at the tertiary level, there must be financial support for the less privileged. Such support should come from government, charities and philanthropists. No desiring and deserving students will be left out.

5. We must pay attention to the education of women because of the disproportionate impact it has on the education of children. If my mother was educated, I am sure that the conversation in my house regarding whether I should go to school would have been different.

6. We must make the right investments to ensure that the material benefits of education are obvious to our youth: jobs, support for small business start-ups and other opportunities for social mobility. If we make the right investments, our youth will not shun education with the excuse that university graduates are increasingly unemployed.

7. Vocational education must be a critical part of the education mix because of its contribution toward helping young people acquire skills targeted at specific jobs.

8. Decentralization of our education policy, planning and management will help improve our education. Basic education should be under local control. The power to control tertiary education should be devolved to state or regional governments. The Federal Government must retain the power to set standards and continue to support states or regions.

I congratulate the Ford Foundation on the 80th anniversary of its work to develop human capacity around the world. I thank the foundation for its important contributions to improve humanity, especially through education and research. Nigeria and Nigerians have benefited enormously from your work and for that, we are immensely grateful.

I urge the Ford Foundation alumni attending this reunion, to imbibe the spirit of giving that has driven the foundation in its work all these years and to give back to society. Your communities need your help; your alma mater needs the help and your country needs your help. I wish you a successful reunion and anniversary celebration.

Thank you.

"The spirit of democracy is not a mechanical thing
To be adjusted by abolition of forms.
It requires a change of heart."

Mahatma Gandhi

16 STRENGTH AND UNITY IN RENEWAL: TOWARDS A REBIRTH OF NIGERIAN FEDERALISM

At the Public Presentation on Nigerian Federalism: Continuing Quest for Stability and Nation-Building, Abuja, 12 December 2016

The structure and practice of Nigerian federalism have been key topics of discussions and debates in Nigeria since the amalgamation of the North and South Protectorates in 1914, with varying levels of intensity.

It is good that this edited work by Okechukwu Ibeanu and Mohammad Kuna is contributing to that debate. I have no illusion that this book, or any other, will settle the issues, but it is an important intervention.

We are all witnesses to the agitations and complaints by different sections of the country at different times about being marginalized or short changed in fiscal allocation and the distribution of such other public resources as political positions, jobs, school admissions, provision of infrastructure, and even social honour. In response, many Nigerians have been calling for some form of restructuring of our federal system, while some small fringe groups insist on their part of the country separating from the federation all together.

Keen observers of those debates and agitations will notice these key tendencies:

1. Those who see restructuring only in terms of so-called resource control, that is, the control of resources by the states from where they are derived. Currently the loudest are from the Niger Delta, where oil revenues, which our government depends on, largely come from.

2. There are those who think that there is an ideal "true federalism" which we must embrace.

3. There are those who argue that federal systems are varied, evolving, and have their specific national and historic characteristics and that what is needed is continued improvement of our federal system.

4. Then there are those who think that the current structure is not the problem, just the managers.

These are all legitimate positions to take in a democracy. What I find odd and somewhat unhelpful is the argument of those who say that we cannot renegotiate our union and who proceed from there to equate every demand for restructuring, with attempts to break up the country. I believe that every form of human relationship is negotiable. Every political relationship is open for negotiations, without pre-set outcomes. As a democrat and businessman, I do not fear negotiations. That is what reasonable human beings do. This is even more important if a stubborn resistance against negotiations can lead to unsavoury outcomes.

I have spoken several times in the past years on the need to restructure our federation in order to devolve more power and resources to the federating units. Recently, I went to Kaduna and told an audience of mostly my compatriots from the North, where most of the resistance against restructuring seems to come from, that restructuring is in the interest of the North and Nigeria. I have even called on states in each geo-political zone to, in the interim, pool their resources together to provide some services for their peoples for greater efficiency and cost effectiveness.

I have limited time here, so I will just make the following observations and remarks.

1. We must acknowledge that what got us to our current over-centralized, and centre-dominated federal system is political expediency and fear, bolstered by the command and control character of military regimes. But after 50 years of 'unitary federalism,' we are now in a position to clearly see that it has not worked well. The federating units in the First Republic had their disagreements but none claimed to lack autonomy of action, and none waited for federal fiscal allocations before it could implement its programs and pay salaries. The current structure may be working for some elites but it has clearly not worked well for any section of this country and the country as a whole. We should take deliberate steps to change this structure to serve us better. And we should not dither for too long, that we let fear and expediency stampede us into another disastrous policy shift that may not serve us well either.

2. We have to acknowledge that federalisms are works in progress: there is no ideal federal system or so-called true federalism. Each nation must work out the best federal system suited for it. In Nigeria's case, we must acknowledge that it is disingenuous, if not outright dishonest, to say that the system is not the problem. If the problem is just the operators, how come we have failed for 50 years to produce the right people? Should we import them from outer space?

   A look at our 1999 Constitution, specifically Section 7, which, as the introduction to this book notes, has 83 legislative items as against 15 for the states (which the Federal Government can also override), shows that there is a huge problem with the system. I challenge anyone who is against restructuring our federation to show me another well-functioning federal system in the world with that level of lopsided central dominance. Individuals operate within certain structural and institutional constraints. If all we lack are good operators, as these people argue, would anyone advocate doing away with constitutions altogether so we rely on fantastic individuals to do the right things?

3. We must acknowledge that agitations for more states across the country, the clamour for more federal take-over of state institutions, and the clamour for local government autonomy (i.e. autonomy from state governments) are inconsistent with establishing a viable and well-functioning federal system. We already have too many weak and unviable states. What we need are stronger federating units (be they existing states or zones), with a greater share of resources and responsibilities.

   I have been shouting myself hoarse asking why we

should have federal roads, federal schools, federal hospitals, etc. I have called for state police, for the states that so desire, to help us provide more effective security. In 2012, I went before ALGON in Enugu and told them that their clamour for local government autonomy from state governments is misguided. I told them that it is wrong for the Federal Government to be creating local governments and giving them money directly from the Federation Account. What is the meaning of "local" then, I asked? How does the transfer of local government dependence on state to central government translate to autonomy?

Even our state governments are nearly totally dependent on the Federal Government, meaning they do not even have the autonomy that we are trying to give to the local governments that are below them. This is a complete absurdity. Can anyone honestly claim that our local governments have performed better since the introduction of the joint state/local government account than they did prior to the coming into effect of that constitutional provision? We must end our culture of institutional escapism in this country. By that, I mean our tendency to create new institutions to solve problems for which we already have institutions just so we avoid dealing with the shortcomings of the existing institutions.

4. We must acknowledge that in federal systems that work, federating units cede certain powers to the centre. In our strange federal contraption, it is the centre that is creating federating units, giving them money and monopolizing most power and resources. Thus, our state governments are no longer performing as federating units. Rather, they currently seem like dependent provinces of the central government in Abuja.

Think about this: sales taxes ought to be collected and used by state and local governments. Of course, there is nothing inherently wrong in a federal sales tax but states must agree with the Federal Government what items should be taxed, at what rate and how the proceeds are to be shared. They ought to be uniform. If a state is opposed to cattle tax or bicycle tax or alcohol tax or pollution tax, for instance, it should not expect to share in the tax proceeds from those items. That is called fairness. In fact, states should be the ones collecting those taxes on behalf of the Federal Government and get compensated for their work, through an agreed sharing formula, rather than duplicating the cost of collection. Federal intrusion makes it more difficult for a state to collect taxes from items that may be peculiar to it, thereby narrowing the tax base. And it makes enforcement even more difficult.

5. No section of this country can claim correctly that its people are better served by the current structure of our federation. When we were not dependent on oil revenues and when the federating units had greater autonomy of action and were largely responsible for their affairs, they, that is, our regional governments did not owe workers their salaries for several months. They did not shut down schools and universities for several months because of teacher strikes and inadequate funding. Look at the industries that the regional governments established and ran and the quality of

schools that they established, and see if you can see a state government or a group of state governments that have bested them since the emergence of our unitary federalism. And ask yourself which of those establishments taken over or established by the Federal Government since, has performed as well as they did under our pre-1966 federal system.

6. National unity does not mean the absence of disagreement or agitations. In fact, disagreements and peaceful agitations indicate vibrant and living relationships. The key to making national progress is to manage those disagreements in peaceful and mature ways.

7. Political and civic leaders from across the country must come together, discuss, negotiate and make the necessary compromises and sacrifices needed to restructure our federation to make us a stronger, more united, productive, and competitive country. Perhaps we might start with making our grievances and fears apparent. When each section or party to a dispute airs its grievances, and expresses its fears and concerns, the outcome may be better understanding by others, and a quicker route to a resolution or agreement. That's perhaps how we should proceed with the much-needed rebirth and renewal of our federation.

I thank the organizers of this public presentation, especially Ambassador S. T. Dogonyaro, for honouring me with the invitation to present the book.

Thank you for your attention.

Bata Dance

"This country was built originally out of negotiations by sectional groups and leaders. I believe that our generation is capable of negotiations and compromises for the greater good of our country and our peoples."

Atiku Abubakar

17 RESTRUCTURING NIGERIA FOR NATIONAL COHESION AND GOOD GOVERNANCE

Delivered at the Third Policy Monitoring Dialogue Series on National Unity, Integration, and Devolution of Power/Restructuring

I have spoken a few times over a long period of time about the need to restructure our federation in order to make it stronger.

Our founding political leaders agreed on and erected a federal system of government. They believed, quite rightly in my view, that such a structure was the only guarantee of national cohesion, in view of our diversity, varying resource endowments, varying levels of development, and the centrifugal forces threatening our unity. Over the years, that structure, which we inherited, has been changed towards greater centralisation of power and concentration of resources at the centre at the expense of the federating units. This has had enormous consequences, including a culture of fiscal dependency of the federating units on the centre, and an over-extended federal government dominating virtually every aspect of our national life. Others are the cries of marginalisation by virtually all segments of our country at different times, the rising din of demands for restructuring, fiscal federalism and even violent extremism. There have also been voices opposed to those demands and agitations.

Definitions

Restructuring, to me, therefore, means effecting changes to our current federal structure to bring it closer to what our founding leaders erected in order to address the very issues and challenges that led them to opt for a less centralised system. It means devolution of more powers to the federating units with the accompanying resources, and it would involve greater control by the federating units of the resources in their areas. It would mean, by implication, the reduction of the powers and roles of the federal government so that it focuses only on those matters best handled by the centre, such as defence, immigration, customs and excise, foreign policy, aviation, as well as setting and enforcing national standards on such matters as education, health and safety.

Good governance, in a democratic setting, would mean that the government effectively and efficiently delivers on its constitutional duties and promises to the electorate in a fair and equitable manner. It also includes meeting other challenges that emerge in the society during the government's tenure. And it includes government being accountable to the people and recognising and effectuating the people's right to know. Thus, transparency is at the core of good governance. Good governance is a requirement for a country's development which, to me, means improving the society's productive capacity, improving the people's welfare and enhancing their freedoms. As we know, governments do not often voluntarily offer transparency, which is why a viable opposition and a vibrant and independent news media are essential ingredients of good governance. Above all, perhaps, good governance requires a vigilant and demanding electorate.

In contemporary Nigeria, good governance would involve addressing the country's economic stagnation and crisis, including transitioning the economy to a post-oil/commodities trajectory, ensuring security, fighting corruption and restructuring the polity, including the structure of the federation and government institutions.

National cohesion refers to a sense of unity and oneness by citizens of a country to the extent that, despite their diversity, they see themselves as forming a nation. That sense of solidarity encourages them to invest economically, socially, politically and emotionally in the wellbeing of the nation-country. National cohesion does not mean the absence of disagreements but that those disagreements play out and are resolved within the parameters laid out by the country's laws and regulations and in a manner that preserves the sense of oneness.

On whether restructuring is the panacea for naational cohesion and good governance: Well, I do not believe that any one single thing is the panacea for national cohesion and good governance in Nigeria, but I have no doubt that effecting the necessary changes to our existing federal structure will help to promote national cohesion and good governance. Some have argued that what our country needs is just good governance, not restructuring. This is misleading. In fact you may have good governance without necessarily having national cohesion, and vice versa. Yes, people want good governance, but often they also want to feel as a part of the governance process. They like to have a sense of belonging. They do not just want to see good governance, they also want fair and equitable governance. And they want to be respected as bona fide members of the society. People like to see themselves represented in those doing the governing. Let's not forget that some of the most efficient and effective governments in history were also exclusionary brutal dictatorships which maintained national cohesion until those regimes collapsed. Equally important is that while restructuring our federal system would help ensure good governance, the latter does not depend on restructuring alone. People and communities at every level must continually demand good governance from their elected officials.

About a week before the last Ramadan, a small business owner in Yola complained to me about how poor power supply was hurting her restaurant business. She wondered why the power situation remains very bad and pleaded with me to do something about it. I explained to her that our country's generation and distribution capacities are not anywhere near enough and that even the little that is generated is sometimes sabotaged by attacks on the pipelines that supply gas to the power plants in the Niger Delta. "Why should we in Yola rely on power from the Niger Delta?", she wondered aloud. "Why can't we have our own power plants in Yola or Adamawa State? Am I supposed to go the Niger Delta to complain?", she fumed.

We should try to understand the basis for the agitations and calls for a new compact, rather than vilifying the agitators. It is disingenuous to accuse everyone who calls for restructuring as trying to break up the country.

I am aware that the current government is working hard to improve the power situation in the country but this woman's questions and statements capture the pitfalls of the excessive centralisation that has been foisted on our country over the years. It must be reversed if we are to set ourselves on a path of sustainable development, peaceful coexistence, and national cohesion.

Ever since the creation of this country out of diverse peoples, cultures, histories and geographies, we have had our differences and conflicts, and early in our history we tried to resolve those differences through negotiations and compromises. Our resolutions were never perfect but they didn't have to be. Human relationships evolve; they change as they seek perfection. Our diversity encouraged our founding leaders to opt for a federal system of the government which they hoped would allow the federating regions the space to control their resources and to develop at their own paces, according to their peculiar situations. At a point in our history, those negotiations and compromises broke down and we had a military take-over of power and subsequently fought a civil war.
Military rule and the civil war led to the steady erosion of our federal structure. The increasing centralisation of power and concentration of resources at the federal level, in the context of rising oil revenues and neglect of other revenue sources, weakened and relatively impoverished the states. As vice president and chairman of the National Privatisation Council (NPC), I saw firsthand what an overly centralised federal government can do wrong. Having confiscated the bulk of national revenues, the federal government proceeded to insert itself in a dominant manner in virtually every aspect of our national life, including the economy where it became an investor in all manner of businesses rather than facilitating the emergence of a vibrant and thriving private sector.

Although we have succeeded in privatising many public enterprises, we still engage in what I call institutional escapism and duplication/ multiplication. Rather than fix existing challenges in existing ministries and departments, we create new ones to carry out the same functions as the existing ones. If the Federal Ministry of Works is not functioning well, we create Federal Roads Maintenance Agency (FERMA). If the police is not doing well with respect to traffic management, we create Federal Road Safety Corps (FRSC). Again we create a Civil Defence Corps in response to the shortcomings of the police in providing security rather than decentralising the police, among other reforms. The list goes on and on. We claim that state governments would abuse state police, yet we hypocritically accept their donations of equipment and funds to the police commands in their states, pretending we don't know that those donations have relational consequences.

As you deliberate, there are three things I suggest you pay serious attention to:

1. People have a constitutional right to peacefully agitate for restructuring, so focus on identifying the reasons for the agitations. We are now in a democracy and democratic freedoms allow people to freely express themselves, including questioning the political and economic structures of the country and their place in it. We should try to understand the basis for the agitations and calls for a new compact, rather than vilifying the agitators. It is disingenuous to accuse everyone who calls for restructuring as trying to break up the country. History tells us that that kind of cheap blackmail will not work as long as the underlying reasons for the agitations persist.

2. It is Ok to have different positions on restructuring. Yes, restructuring may mean different things to different people. Like all things with political and economic implications, those calling for restructuring have varying positions, which is not a bad thing. But we won't really find out how close our positions are to those of others until we sit down with them and start to talk and negotiate. The biggest challenge seems to be that we appear to be allowing moderate voices on this issue to be drowned out by the reckless utterances of a few rabble rousers on all sides, who may be tools in the hands of those who do not wish this country well. These are some of the people who arrogate to themselves the toga of spokespersons of our diverse groups.

3. Restructuring will contribute to national cohesion and good governance. I have no doubt that restructuring our federal system would contribute the following, among other things:

a. Devolving more powers to the federating units and transferring more resources to them will help to decongest the centre and enhance greater manageability, efficiency and accountability. There will be more clarity in the division of powers and responsibilities between the centre and the federating units, and there will be a reduction in the attention paid to the centre. In my view, there should be no federal roads, therefore states will be responsible for road construction and maintenance and people will know that. The same would go for schools and hospitals. State police (for states that so desire) will help improve security. States that do not want their own police forces will work out arrangements with the federal authorities over cost-sharing for policing in their jurisdictions. The key thing is that federating units will have greater resources, authority and capacity to tackle localised problems with national impact, including education, health care, roads and insecurity, such as the herdsmen-farmers clashes, armed robbery, kidnapping, militancy and other forms of insecurity that may manifest themselves as cultism or other anti-social behaviours. That would be good governance. And the incentive for states in a region or zone to pool together to provide services will be stronger when we pull the federal government out of direct involvement in these. And there's nothing that says we must maintain a 36-state structure. We obviously can't go back to the former regions because of minority rights concerns. So, we should explore the option of using the geo-political zones as federating units. With devolved powers and resources, they will be more viable than the existing states. And their current make-up is more suited to addressing minority concerns.

b. Restructuring will ensure greater accountability. People are more likely to hold their state and local governments to account once those governments are no longer able to convincingly blame the central government for their shortcomings.

c. Restructuring will promote healthy competition among our federating units, which will encourage them to diversify their revenue sources.

d. Restructuring will ensure greater fairness and a perception of same among our constituent parts.

e. Beyond these, there is also another huge economic

imperative for us to restructure: Oil, which underlined and underwrote our excessive centralisation and fragmentation into numerous unviable states, and which has been at the centre of much of our squabbles, seems to have reached its peak as a source of revenues for our country. In fact, long-term, it seems to be on a downward trajectory. And even if its contribution to our revenues were to remain at current levels in the long term, it still spells trouble for our economy and the unsustainable structure which it has supported for nearly 50 years. The states or zones of the country that are most dependent on oil revenues have a greater urgency to decouple themselves from that dependency now that there is still some oil revenue to assist them in the transition. That window may not remain open for a long time, which may then make the inevitable transition much more painful and chaotic. New technologies of oil production have hugely increased oil output, especially in the US. This, as well as the massive investments in alternative energy sources around the world, has depressed oil prices. And things are going to get worse for oil dependent economies. Norway has announced a ban on the sale of fossil fuel powered cars from 2025. France will ban the sale of such vehicles from 2040. And Volvo has just announced that every new model of car that it would produce from 2019 – in just two years' time – will be either wholly electric or hybrid. Tesla, the American maker of electric vehicles, just started the production of its soon-to-be mass-produced Model 3, just as other vehicle manufacturers are joining the bandwagon.

We must be open-minded as we debate issues of restructuring and as we approach negotiations on it. Sponsoring so-called youth groups to issue provocative statements and cause trouble is not a substitute for reasoned arguments on the better path to the future. This country was built originally out of negotiations by sectional groups and leaders. I believe that our generation is capable of negotiations and compromises for the greater good of our country and our peoples.

Ekpo Masquerade

"let me caution us all that restructuring, by whatever name, is not a magic bullet that would resolve all of Nigeria's challenges or those of any section, region or zone of the country."

Atiku Abubakar

18 RESTRUCTURING FOR A UNITED AND PROGRESSIVE NIGERIA

Speech by Atiku Abubakar, GCON, former Vice President, Federal Republic of Nigeria, at the University of Nigeria, Nsukka, Wednesday 19th July, 2017.

Let me begin with a rhetorical question: why do I, Atiku Abubakar, favour a restructured Nigeria? The answer is simple: because I am proudly Nigerian and favour a united Nigeria that offers every man, woman and child a brighter future where each and everyone has a chance to build and share in this great nation's potential.

The Restructuring I want to see happen is changing the structure of our country to take power from the elite and give it back to whom it belongs: the people. It will help to bring the benefits of the change that our people were promised in the last general elections.

For a number of years now we have been making the case for the restructuring of our federal system. This is in response to the cries of marginalisation by various segments of country as well as the understanding that our federation, as presently constituted, impedes optimal development and the realization of our peoples' aspirations. As you all know, virtually every segment of this country has at one point or the other complained of marginalisation by one or more segments, and agitated for change.

Before I proceed, let me caution us all that restructuring, by whatever name, is not a magic bullet that would resolve all of Nigeria's challenges or those of any section, region or zone of the country. Listening to some people, even those who seek to dismember the country, you would think that once their dream is achieved their part of the country or the country as a whole will become paradise.

Yet, as we all know, life is not that simple. We need restructuring in order to address the challenges that hold us back and which restructuring alone can help us address, and which will remain unaddressed unless we restructure. Period. This also answers the cynics who question whether restructuring is even important since it won't solve all our problems. No system would.

To me, restructuring means making changes to our current federal structure so it comes closer to what our founding leaders established, in response to the very issues and challenges that led them to opt for a less centralized system.

Perhaps it is because I spent a decade in the private sector before coming back to the public sector as Vice President that I have the benefit of a paradigm that sees opportunity where others see crisis, but that is my world view.

The issue of restructuring is beyond resource control. There are other and even more important issues in this whole debate which I will address in this speech, but as resource control seems to be the one issue that many blocs are fixated on, let me take some time to address it first.

My vision of Restructuring, will not make some States richer and others poorer. Restructuring is a win win for all Nigerian states.

So let me make it clear beyond any possible doubt: the Restructuring I am proposing will not reduce the share of our nation's oil revenues that any state currently enjoys. However if we are to grow our revenues we need to change the way we think of our resources and nurture them for the benefit of all.

So let us start by not thinking as if our resources consist only of oil. Oil is not infinite. In fact, within the industry, the oil majors and multi-nationals are looking for ways to further invest in alternative energy because in the next 10-20 years the proportion of the energy market share that fossil fuels hold will shrink and almost vanish even as those of alternative energy are set to rise dramatically.

Automobile manufacturers such as Volvo and Peugeot have announced plans to phase out petrol and diesel cars. This is not a conspiracy. It is a fact. The man just elected as France's President, Emmanuel Macron, has told the world that petrol and diesel cars will be illegal to make or sell in France by 2040. Norway has said it will do the same but earlier: by 2025.

On a recent visit to the United Kingdom I noticed that senior members of the Conservative Party were driving the Toyota Mirai, a car that runs on hydrogen and emits water instead of harmful carbon monoxide. Professor Tony Seba, a world renowned global economist, has published his findings that all new cars will be electric by 2025.

So the world is not waiting for us to see reason and reengineer our economy. If we do, they will work with us. If we do not, the world will leave us behind.

For the last decade, Nigeria has made an average of $30 billion per annum from oil. This may look like a lot of money, but when you factor in our population of close to 200 million people growing at one of the highest rates in the world at 2.6% per annum, that money starts to look relatively small. We must begin to look for other and more sustainable sources of income that are also realistic.

Africa, especially sub Saharan Africa, imports 82% of her food from outside the continent. Every year, Africa spends $35.4 billion on food imports from Europe, Asia and America.

I have been to virtually all the world's continents and to many of her nations, and scientists everywhere agree with what the International Institute of Tropical Agriculture (IITA) says, that Africa and particularly Nigeria has some of the most fertile soils on planet earth. Why can't most of that $35.4 billion, which is bigger than our annual revenues from oil, come to Nigeria instead? It is not coming now because our focus is on how to share the $30 billion we get from oil every year and when your focus is on sharing, you cannot be creative.

The whole purpose of Restructuring is to eliminate those policies that feed the mindset that drives the sharing behaviour so that we can have a paradigm shift towards a mindset that drives creative and productive behaviour.

We do not have to look too far. We are already seeing it in Nigeria.

I just told you that I was recently in the U.K. One of the things I learned on that visit is that Britain is very pleased with the increase in vegetable imports from Nigeria especially pumpkin leaves. You in the Southeast call it ugu. One state, Anambra, has decided to take her share of the $35.4 billion Africa spends importing food and is now exporting ugu to other nations including the U.K.

Some oil producing states are owing workers' salary, Anambra is not owing. A number of oil producing states took the Federal Government bailout, Anambra did not take it. Anambra state is proof that restructuring is good for our states and will not bankrupt them.

If Anambra, a state that suffers from soil erosion and has a very high population density, can export £5 million worth of pumpkin leaves to foreign nations, 1 million tubers of yam to Europe and millions of dollars-worth of scent leaves, locally known as nchanw, then much larger states like Kano, Borno, Kaduna, Kwara, Ogun and Rivers should be able to do even more.

The time has come to say the truth. Whilst it might be inconvenient for our elite who are the ones profiting from the oil rent economy and the feeding bottle of our current deformed federalism, I believe we need to speak the truth. And the truth is this: our national wealth is being drained by a select few instead of building a country for all of us. It has to end. We need to return resources and power back to the local level, and from the elite to the people.

Only by restructuring can we guarantee Unity, Equity and Security for our nation.

Along with the late great Chief M.K.O Abiola, I was a member of the former Social Democratic Party. The party's manifesto included the following words, to 'improve the people's welfare and fight for social justice'. We in the SDP were the progressives. We were the party of Olu Falae, of Shehu Musa Yar'adua, of Abubakar Rimi, of Jim Nwobodo and of Bola Tinubu.

So it surprises me today, and perhaps even shocks me that anybody that was elected on or connected to that platform would say he or she does not know what restructuring means.

I am proud to say that the SDP invented restructuring as it pertains to Nigeria. Our Presidential candidate was a pan Nigerian patriot who promised to restructure the country. Anybody connected to that platform should be seen as making the case for restructuring simpler rather than complicating it.

Quick Wins

When people hear the term restructuring, all sorts of emotions are evoked. Why is this so? Some feel a sense of impending triumph; others feel a sense of impending loss and defeat. But it doesn't have to be so. If our people see that restructuring will benefit all of us, some of the contentions will abate. We can move quickly to demonstrate some of those benefits with those aspects of restructuring that do not require constitutional amendment.

Take education and roads for instance. The federal government can immediately start the process of transferring federal roads to the state governments along with the resources it expends on them. In the future if the federal government identifies the need for a new road that would serve the national interest, it can support the affected states to construct such roads. Thereafter the maintenance would be left to the states, which can collect tolls from road users for that purpose. The federal government does not need a constitutional amendment to start that process.

We do not need a constitutional amendment to transfer federal universities and colleges as well as hospitals to the states where they are located. The University of Nigeria, Nsukka, the Ahmadu Bello University, Zaria and the University of Ife (now OAU) were built by regional governments when we had a thriving federal system. We all know what then happened. The federal government, awash in oil revenues, took them over, rapidly expanded them, and began to build more federal universities in response to the inevitable demand from states that did not have any located within their jurisdictions. Without adequate and sustainable funding the result is what we have today: universities, including the first generation ones that are no longer taken seriously anywhere in the world.

Yet many of our young people cannot find spaces in our tertiary institutions. This year alone, 1.7 million Nigerians wrote the 2017 Unified Tertiary Matriculation Examinations. Last year the figure was 1.5 million.

According to the Nigerian Bureau of Statistics and the Joint Admissions and Matriculation Board, of the 10 million Nigerian youths who wrote the UTME since 2010, only 26% gained admission into Nigerian universities. That left out 74% that could not get in. This gross inadequacy of school spaces breeds corruption in the admissions process and sustains our perennial fights over quota system and the like. A decentralized system is unlikely to be that insensitive to the yearnings of the people and the needs of the economy. We must reverse the epidemic of federal take-over of state and voluntary organizations' schools and hospitals which began in the 1970s, and also transfer those established by the federal government to the states.

Last year, 60,000 Nigerian students spent 300 billion Naira on education in Ghanaian universities. In that same period 18,000 of our youths spent 162 billion Naira in the U.K. Altogether, Nigerians spend a yearly average of 1 trillion Naira on foreign education because we do not have enough capacity to meet demand.

We must find a way to keep that 1 trillion Naira on our shores by investing it in building enough educational capacity for our own people and a quality of education which all our neighbours would aspire to. Think of the impact retaining 1 trillion Naira in our economy will have for the value of the Naira.

But why are we not already doing this? I do it in my own private university. I have seen the benefits. The American University of Nigeria at Yola has students from all over the world because we have invested in capacity.

Education is a priority. Of course when we are spending hundreds of billions on needless luxuries and on fighting yesterday's wars we will not have the 1 trillion naira to spend on education. Nations do not become wealthy by having state of the art luxuries. They become wealthy by having state of the art schools.

Enough of that issue. Let us go to the next level.

The excessive concentration of power and centralization of resources in the federal government led the government to extend itself into virtually every aspect of our lives including as an investor in an array of businesses. And almost as a rule they were badly run. The reason is because we have made our government into an enterprise rather than a service. We no longer have civil servants in the true sense of the word. Our civil service is more lucrative than the private sector such that when people see a nice house or a fancy car they automatically think it must belong to a top government official.

For twenty seven years I have been a proponent of privatisation. I was the head of the National Council on Privatisation and I know for a fact that if you privatise all the enterprises that government unnecessarily controls such as the NNPC, NRC, you will reduce the mad scramble for control of federal power and patronage positions in those organizations.

I oversaw the bidding round for new telecommunications licenses in 2000. It is on record that Nigeria had the most transparent bidding process in the world then. We generated $1.2 billion for the federal government and liberalised the mobile telecommunications industry which resulted in an increase from 500,000 lines to 100 million lines.

So privatisation took the power of telephony from our elites who could pay 10,000 Naira for a SIM card and placed it firmly in the palms of the people of Nigeria. Today a SIM card is virtually given away for free and the power of telephony is in all our hands. It also had the benefit of directly generating employment for over 100,000 Nigerians in the new telcos and literally hundreds of thousands more indirectly via the resellers who sit under umbrellas at street corners selling recharge cards.

Privatisation and liberalisation create wealth and opportunity with little regard to where you come from. Which brings me to the economic aspect of restructuring. Nigeria is blessed with huge oil and gas deposits, but we will not become wealthy by merely selling more crude oil or more LNG. Our wealth must be tied to the productive capacity of our people. What is in our brains beats what is in our grounds.

Let us not be afraid of any state controlling their resources as long as they pay the agreed taxes to the center. Let us rather be afraid of being so fixated on oil that we do not even see the wealth that is under our noses, and fail to realize when oil ceases to be that important.

As I mentioned earlier, oil is getting more and more redundant. We must turn our energies towards developing a real economy and not an economy based on rent seeking.

Before the discovery of oil in commercial quantities, the Saudi Royal Family received medical treatment from the University College Hospital, Ibadan. More than 50 years after the discovery of oil in commercial quantities our own leaders now depend on others for their healthcare.

Why has this happened? In my opinion, it is because we got drunk on oil. We need to go to rehab. And if resource control, within reason, will do that for us, then we should stop resisting it and start embracing it.

Addressing restructuring along the lines I and other like-minded patriots have suggested will not be the solution to all the symptoms of the disease of insufficient capacity plaguing Nigeria. However it will be the critical first step to tackling Nigeria's various diseases.

So let me now turn to the critical issue of security facing our nation's unity and the wellbeing of our people.

By devolving power to the States and local governments, the federal government equips them with the resources, authority and capacity to tackle local problems that has national significance. In this way it will help solve the issue of herdsmen-farmers clashes, kidnapping, militancy and other forms of insecurity that may manifest themselves as cultism or other anti-social behaviours. We should do more than merely ordering the police or the military to crush terrorists, kidnappers, cultists and separatists. We must also address the environment that allowed such issues to erupt in the first place. If you pull out the leaves of weeds without removing the weeds by the roots, they will grow again.

I believe that the benefits accruing from these first steps will help us as we move towards the changes that require amendments to our Constitution. Let me mention a few critical ones just to illustrate.

a. Creation of and Funding of Local Governments by the Federal Government. Few things illustrate federal overreach into state matters than the creation and direct funding of local governments by the Federal Government. As I have said on numerous occasions, this makes a mockery of the word "local." No good evidence has been produced to show that our local governments are now doing better than they were prior to federal intrusion. That intrusion must stop. Local governments are not federating units. State governments should have the freedom to create as many local governments as they wish or not have local governments at all. Citizens at every locality would then know that it is the responsibility of their states to provide services for their welfare. A possible compromise to help reduce opposition to this needed change is for the existing number of local governments to be maintained during the transition with the federal funds going the respective states as part of devolution of resources. Henceforth local government administration should be the responsibility of state governments.

b. A constitutional amendment allowing for the establishment of State Police is another critical element of the required restructuring. With that, the Federal and state governments should be able to decide on jurisdictions and which matters would fall under federal statutes and which under state statutes, and where there would be joint jurisdiction (in which case the federal government can take over in cases of conflict). One thing about federalism that we seem to have forgotten is that it is about freedom, autonomy and choice. State police would not be mandatory for every state. Those states which, for whatever reason, prefer federal police would work out arrangements with the federal police on cost-sharing and other matters related to policing their jurisdictions.

c. Reduction in the Number of Federating Units. I strongly

believe that we need to reduce the number of federating units. The decades of excessive reliance on oil revenues and the relative neglect of other revenue sources as well as our near addiction to states-creation mean that even the increase of the resources transferred to the states may not make many of the financially non-viable states to become viable. Those calling for new states seem oblivious of the fiscal crisis the existing states are in and how dependent they are on transfer payments from Abuja. If we are to maintain the current state structure, how do we ensure their financial viability? Obviously they would have to diversify their economies and revenue sources, but what happens to those unable to do so? One option that I have suggested is a means-test requiring states to generate a specified percentage of their share of federal allocations internally or be absolved into another state. Or we may revisit Chief Alex Ekwueme's suggestion that we use the existing geopolitical zones as federating units rather than the current states. Using the zones would ensure immediate financial viability and scale and also address the concerns of minorities about domination by our three major ethnic groups.

d. The issue of Resource Control is perhaps the most contentious. It is the big elephant in the room but the one most proponents and opponents of restructuring prefer to dance around while often throwing insults at each other. Fear, greed, envy, and resentment are at the centre of our disagreements on resource control. On the one hand, those who feel they are better endowed with the currently important or exploited national resource, oil, express some level of greed and resentment and a desire to monopolize those resources. On the other hand, those who feel less well-endowed express some degree of fear, envy and resentment. We must start from the point of view that no country's regions or localities are equally or uniformly endowed. Diversity is the norm, and often the strength. And there are also historical swings or changes in fortune: the well-endowed areas of today may become less so tomorrow. Sharing is part of human existence and part of what makes human societies possible. I have consistently advocated for local control of resources but with federal taxing powers to help redistribute resources and to help address national priorities. Local control will encourage our federating units to look inwards at untapped resources in their respective domains and promote healthy rivalry among them.

I must point out that all of these do not have to be done in one fell swoop. We recognise that fundamental change is often difficult, especially for those who feel that they are beneficiaries of the status quo. But we must change. We cannot keep doing the same thing and expect a different outcome.

We can start with the less contentious ones, including state police, and returning jurisdiction for local governments to states.

Discussions and negotiations among leaders from across the country can be speeded up to ensure timely resolution of these contentious issues. Our generation cannot afford to be the one that is unable to negotiate and bargain for a workable federal system that truly serves our peoples and enables them to live in peace and harmony with mutual respect.

The Nigerian federation is a work in progress. We just have to continue that work, a truly serious work, to build bridges across our various divides. That's what we need in order to create the kind of country where our young people can thrive and realize their full potentials, young people such as Ms Immaculata Onuigbo, the best graduating student and Valedictorian for the Class of 2017 at the American University Nigeria, Yola. We owe it to them and the generations to come.

I thank the Senior Staff Club of the UNN for inviting me to share these thoughts with you and for honouring me today.

Thank you for your attention and may God bless Nigeria.

Old Residency Building and Calabar Museum, Calabar, Cross River State.

"The Nigerian federation is a work in progress. We just have to continue that work, a truly serious work, to build bridges across our various divides. That's what we need in order to create the kind of country where our young people can thrive and realise their full potential. Our generation cannot afford to be the one that is unable to negotiate and bargain for a workable federal system that truly serves our peoples and enables them to live in peace and harmony and mutual respect."

Atiku Abubakar